An Evening with Venus

An Evening with Venus

Prostitution during the American Civil War

John Gaines

State House Press

Press

Buffalo Gap, Texas

Library of Congress Cataloging-in-Publication Data

Gaines, John Jackson
An Evening With Venus: Prostitution during the American Civil War
John Gaines
    p. cm.
Includes Bibliographical references and index.
ISBN 978-1-933337-62-3 (pbk. alk. paper)
ISBN- 933337-62-1 (pbk. alk. paper)
1. History United States 2. History / Civil War Period (1850-1877) 3. United
States: History-20th century. 4. HISTORY / United States/State & Local/
Southwest (AZ, NM, OK, TX) 5. HISTORY / United States/State & Local/
South (AL, AR, FL, GA, KY, LA, MS, NC, SC, TN)
This paper meets the requirements of ANSI/NISO, Z39.48-1992 (permanence
of paper) Binding materials have been chosen for durability ♻ ∞
I. Title.
    "Cataloging-in-Publication Data available from the Library of Congress"

State House Press
P.O. Box 818
Buffalo Gap, Texas 79508
325-572-3974 · 325-572-3991 (fax)
www.tfhcc.com

Printed in the United States of America
Distributed by Texas A&M University Press Consortium
800-826-8911
www.tamupress.com

ISBN-13: 978-1-933337-62-3
ISBN-10: 1-933337-62-1

Book Design by Rosenbohm Graphic Design

Contents

Acknowledgments

As with any project of this magnitude, this book would not have been possible without the help and encouragement that I have received from a great many people.

The staff members of the various libraries and archives have been instrumental in aiding my location of source materials. I am particularly indebted to DeAnne Blanton of the National Archives and Records Administration as well as Conni Kitten of the Interlibrary Loan Office at the University Library at Texas Tech. Both Blanton and Kitten went out of their way to provide invaluable assistance in locating even the most cursory references.

I am also appreciative of those historians who researched topics in sexuality before me. Because of them, the subject is a more acceptable avenue of research. Although still somewhat risqué, I have received nothing but support from academics and others with who I have shared the project.

I have an immense amount of gratitude for Alwyn Barr for his thorough reviews and suggestions as the manuscript took shape. His willingness to review unending drafts and attention to detail has allowed the work to achieve its current state. Appreciation is also warranted for Paul Carlson, Julie Willett, and Jeffrey Mosher who offered critical appraisal and guidelines during the early stages of the project. Also deserving of thanks are the great people at the McWhiney History Education Group and State House Press. Scott Clowdus, Director of Operations, Donald S. Frazier, President and CEO, and Claudia Gravier Frigo, project manager, have all been immensely helpful in bringing this project to fruition.

Finally, my thanks go to my wife, Michelle, and my son William. They have offered tremendous support and numerous welcome distractions throughout work on the book. They have given me the direction to see this book through to the conclusion. I will always love you both.

Introduction

In September 1865, President Andrew Johnson wrote a letter to Major General George H. Thomas, who was the commander of the Military Division of Tennessee. Johnson expressed concern about the activities of African American troops in East Tennessee. According to Johnson, the soldiers:

> have even gone so far as to have taken my own house and converted it into a rendezvous for male and female negroes, who have been congregated there, in fact making it a common negro brothel. It was bad enough to be taken by traitors and converted into a rebel hospital, but a negro whore house is infinitely worse. As to the value of the property, I care nothing for that, but the reflection that it has been converted into a sink of pollution, and that by our own forces is, I confess, humiliating in the extreme.[1]

The president went on to suggest that if the African American soldiers in East Tennessee could not be brought under control, that "[I]t would be far better to remove every negro soldier from East Tennessee, and leave the people to protect themselves as best they may."[2] Although this suggestion seems quite melodramatic, the citizens of the region did not face any serious threats. The war had been over for nearly five months; and as a Unionist area, East Tennessee did not require the presence of Union soldiers to enforce the law.

Johnson's most pressing concern was the idea of his home being occupied by African Americans. Until the war, Johnson owned seven to ten slaves. In light of his role as a slave owner, it is understandable that Johnson became infuriated at the prospect of people, whom he viewed in the same class as property, occupying his home.

However, Johnson's letter is a subject of controversy. Although the president truly believed that his former home was being used as an African American brothel, whether or not the house served that purpose is a matter of debate.[3] Johnson's belief about the use his home being disputed by historians is telling about larger ideas of prostitution during the Civil War. Both government agencies and the general public have purposely ignored, and at times, have worked to eradicate evidence of prostitution during the war. For many Americans—Northerners and Southerners—a rumor that their ancestors consorted with prostitutes is a terrible embarrassment. Efforts to edit family history and avoid the embarrassment have unfortunately led to the destruction of letters and diary pages that refer to soldiers and ladies of the evening with whom the soldiers may or may not have been intimate. According to historian Burke Davis, family members "became impassioned censors who weeded out most signs of the bawdy life of the war years."[4]

At one point, the US military worked to maintain the "moral and virtuous" reputations of the soldiers. Shortly after the conclusion of the war, the Office of the Adjutant General began compiling a file on a rather well-known prostitute named Annie Jones. Jones associated with several Union officers, including Judson Kilpatrick and George A. Custer, who later denied an intimate relationship with her. In 1879, John Labine requested Jones's folder. A staff member from the office replied: "It is not deemed advisable or conducive to the public interest to supply the copies requested." Eventually, the National Archives came into possession of the file, but it was not until after World War II that Jones's story became known to historians of the period.[5]

Over the last several decades, historians have become much more inclusive in their studies of the past. Not only have they departed from the "great white man" emphasis in US history and begun to focus on other races and women, but they have also have given more consideration to the working class in a broader view of history. Although previous interpretations of events did not examine the impoverished and laboring classes, women, or other races to much extent, the historians who constructed the picture did so with records left by officers, politicians, and others of the upper and middle classes. The quieter voices of many other historical figures—the less educated, the working class, minorities, and women—were ignored for the most part because of the perceived inadequacies and scarce nature of their writings. Fortunately, later generations of historians have begun to reconstruct the collective lives of those groups through the use of quantitative sources and public records.

Another trend that made possible this book is the acceptance of social history within a military context. In the twenty-first century, the history of the American Civil War no longer concerns only soldiers, battles, politics, and generals but also the privations on the home front, the lives of children during the war, the histories of towns and cities following battles, as well as "the Girl I Left Behind," or in the case of this book, "the Girl I'm Visiting Tonight."

Ultimately, the inclusion of social histories by military historians, the more creative use of evidence, and the support of sexuality as a valid historical subject have combined to endorse the pursuit of this book on prostitution during the Civil War. Nearly everyone with whom I have discussed the project offered enthusiastic interest—historian and non-historian alike.

The title, *An Evening with Venus: Prostitution during the American Civil War*, is an effort to forestall any romantic images of the sex trade that may come to the reader on first impression. Present-day readers likely view an encounter with a sex worker to be a romanticized, yet taboo affair—quite possibly much the same way that the potential customers of the prostitutes during the Civil War did. Ultimately, however, the incident abounded with risks of violence or disease as well as the central issue of the woman conducting a business transaction concerning her survival (rather than being honestly attracted to the customer).

Curiously, other professional historians have only touched on the subject of prostitution during the Civil War. Bell I. Wiley's seminal works, *The Life of Johnny Reb* and *The Life of Billy Yank*, only consider prostitution on 11 of the total 454 pages. Reid Mitchell's follow-up work, *Civil War Soldiers*, only mentions the subject on 1 of the 274 pages. More recently however, Thomas P. Lowry, a lay historian, addressed the topic in *The Story the Soldiers Wouldn't Tell: Sex in the Civil War*. Although Lowry focused on prostitution and venereal disease in some chapters, his account is a narrative history with limited analysis.[6]

The most thoughtful look at prostitution during the war, Catherine Clinton's *Public Women and the Confederacy* (1999), originated as one of a series of lectures. Clinton stated that the purpose of her address was to draw increased attention to prostitution and ultimately to inspire other historians to further examine the subject. Her essays pointed to several different areas of Civil War prostitution that demand examination: various categories of sex work, the possible effects of disease on the war effort, conflicting reactions by officers, and various attempts at quelling the sex trade in larger cities. Clinton rightly stated that the Civil War brought about the largest increase in sex workers in the nineteenth century because of the widespread hardship during the war. Such engagement in the sex trade unfortunately brought into question the morality of women in the Civil War era as a whole. In her call for further research, Clinton presented a complex picture of sex work, wartime chaos, and morality.[7] In response to Clinton's call, this book will analyze more fully the causes and impact of prostitution during the Civil War.

Scholars have offered helpful insights as they explored the sex trade in other time periods of US history. Focusing on the years leading up to the Civil War, Christine Stansell examined the various methods that women used to survive or obtain luxuries in antebellum New York City. Stansell discussed the practice of "occasional prostitution," that is, periodically picking up a client or two for the purposes of obtaining some extra money or more often to correct an economic shortfall while holding a "traditional" occupation. Sexual commerce offered a means of self-sufficiency and an avenue of escape from abusive households.[8]

According to Stansell, in addition to practicing prostitution as a method of self-sufficiency, sex also became a part of other occupations. Domestic workers and other wage-earning females worked in sometimes dangerous locations. Like male slave owners in the South, employers held a great deal of power over their domestic servants. With no one to offer assistance in a private home, domestics frequently became victims of rape and other abuse.[9] With feelings of victimization and survivor's guilt, some domestics left that form of employment and turned to prostitution as a means of livelihood as well as taking back control, to a degree, of their sexuality.

Timothy Gilfoyle's work on prostitution in New York complements Stansell's study. Gilfoyle offered an examination of the sex trade from the colonial period through 1920, documenting the changes and consistencies within prostitution.[10] Victoria Bynum's examination of sexuality in the South during the antebellum period granted a foundation for the gender norms that served as a backdrop for prostitution during the Civil War.[11] This book will employ Stansell, Gilfoyle, and Bynum's concepts to understand women involved in the sex trade, especially in those cities enduring skyrocketing inflation. Hunger and desperation became incredible motivators for the loosening of morals and corsets.

Anne Butler's work, *Daughters of Joy, Sisters of Misery: Prostitutes in the American West, 1865–90*, documented the lives of prostitutes following the Civil War. Butler provided a comprehensive analysis of the relationships that prostitutes had with each other. Similar impoverished economic circumstances led most of them to what the middle class viewed as a sordid occupation, which created some camaraderie among the women. This became evident in instances of a prostitute's death because her coworkers pooled their resources to pay for a coffin and funeral service. Yet prostitutes in a brothel or along the street worked in direct economic competition with each other. Court records document women stealing money and valuables from each other. In several cases prostitutes fought and even killed each other for the attentions of a favored customer.[12] Though Butler wrote about sex workers in the years following the war and in a different part of the country, she argued that prostitution during the nineteenth century served as an occupation of survival during a time of limited options for women.

Ruth Rosen explored Progressive reformers in *The Lost Sisterhood: Prostitution in America, 1900–1918.* Some groups continued from the Civil War period to function as reformers during the Progressive Era; other groups established themselves during the early twentieth century. With little regard for the economic futures and narrow opportunities for the women, those reformers enthusiastically closed brothel districts and encouraged prostitutes to adopt traditional women's work such as sewing or washing clothing, both which usually paid far below subsistence wages.[13] Efforts by the Young Men's Christian Association (YMCA), the Magdalen Society, and the US Christian Commission that attempted to uphold the morals of soldiers by working against the numerous opportunities to engage in vice during the Civil War will be analyzed with Rosen's conclusions in mind.

Butler, Stansell, and Rosen offer interpretations of prostitution claiming that the trade worked to bridge the economic needs or desires of women in areas where men typically outnumbered women. All three historians agree that prostitution—occasional or full-time—did not prove to be a sound decision, although for many of these women it seemed to be one of the only available avenues. Their insights will be applied to sex workers during the Civil War.

This book explores a wide variety of subjects relating to prostitution during the Civil War. It consists of seven chapters, with each exploring a related but slightly different facet of the topic. Taken as a whole, it attempts to offer a more complete picture of the sex trade during the Civil War.

Chapter 1, Morality and Prostitution in Antebellum America, clarifies the basis of social mores concerning gender and sexuality in the years just before the Civil War. Although previous historians have examined this aspect of society, it is important to place the contradictions and continuities of Victorian morality in the context of the emerging war. Issues of class, religion, and race all served to shape the viewpoints of politicians, officers, and enlisted men with regard to the ways in which they reacted to the sex trade during the war.

The first chapter is followed by four chapters that offer analyses of prostitutes, enlisted men, officers, reformers, and medical professionals. Though some figures fall into more than one of these categories, the breakdown represents the four major groups involved in struggles over the sex trade during the war.

Chapter 2, addressing prostitutes, examines both the morality and economics behind women in prostitution. Some women made the conscious decision to forsake society's morals and sell their bodies, but far many more women gradually compromised social norms while working both at a traditional job and as an occasional prostitute to supplement their income. Along with the transformation of morals, this chapter will also address prostitution from an economic point of view, with consideration of race and class. Because many women did not have sufficient employment prospects, the loss of a husband (either through temporary military service or death) often forced them to make a choice between their own starvation, and possibly that of their children, and turning to a life of vice.

Where would prostitutes be without customers? Chapter 3 examines the clientele of the Cyprians. Enlisted men made up the bulk of the clientele for "wayward" women. Because of the physical demands placed on the fighting men of both armies—then as later—the soldiers were mostly young men inexperienced in the ways of the world. Understanding that death was possible, many of the men in both armies sought to experience as much of life as possible before facing a morbid eventuality. Another motivation for seeking out Cyprians appeared because of the widely held feeling that the war was a grand adventure. Communities staged parades and celebrations for departing soldiers, who were likely to continue the celebration with boyhood friends at the first city they entered. Not all enlisted men sought the company of prostitutes or other vices for comfort. These men are included in the chapter on reformers because they often attempted to safeguard the moral standing of their fellow soldiers. Again, race, class, and religion will be discussed.

Chapter 4 discusses the efforts of officers who attempted to keep their men away from prostitutes for reasons of middle-class morality and venereal diseases. Other officers believed that as long as visits to such women did not interfere with the duties of their men, there was no reason to interfere. Because no military regulations addressed the question at the time, officers were left to their own discretion as to whether to allow their men to patronize prostitutes. Although some officers attempted to eradicate the sex trade among their charges, others came fairly close to regulation of prostitution with the programs at Nashville and Memphis. Furthermore, although the issue of their men visiting prostitutes raised concerns among some officers, other officers chose to consort with the women themselves.

Immorality and disease became great concerns to the reformers and medical professionals of the period, which is the subject of Chapter 5. Chapter 5 begins by addressing a chief concern for participants and reformers, venereal diseases. The two diseases that became most prevalent among partakers in the sex trade were gonorrhea and syphilis. A detailed discussion of the symptoms, eventual outcomes, and most importantly, the contemporary methods of treatment and their effectiveness are included in this chapter. Unfortunately for the men, and future sexual partners, medical cures of the period either masked the symptoms, or at worse, poisoned the patient and caused neurological damage. Following the description of disease, the chapter turns to moral reformers. Some reformers, such as members of the Magdalen Society, attempted to rescue prostitutes by rehabilitating them using moral lessons and job training, which was often in low-paying occupations such as laundress or seamstress. Other groups sought to ensure the moral safety of men through a variety of means. The US Christian Commission attempted to prevent soldiers from receiving obscene materials through the mail; they also held religious services in an attempt to discourage soldiers from relying on vice for entertainment. The "Ironsides Regiment," a loosely organized group of soldiers affiliated with the New York YMCA, included upstanding young men who depended on each other for moral support. Although they had various motivations and methodologies, the goal of the reformers was clear: to keep the boys away from the girls.

The last two chapters are case studies of cities in which the military and sex trade played prominent roles. Washington, D.C., Richmond, Virginia, and Nashville and Memphis, Tennessee, all had municipal organizations concerned with prostitution. The cities differed, however, because of region and the groups controlling those organizations. Municipal governments controlled Washington, D.C., and Richmond for the duration of the war, except for the final days in Richmond. City and Confederate authorities initially controlled Nashville and Memphis until they were lost to federal forces in 1862. Nashville, also known as the "Athens of the South," then became the first city in the United States in which prostitution was legalized. Setting aside issues of morality, the Union provost guard of Nashville engaged in an attempt to control the spread of venereal diseases, which the US military in Memphis would emulate.

Ultimately, the goal of this book is to describe and analyze more fully a largely overlooked aspect of the American Civil War. Prostitution became a major concern throughout the Civil War in terms of both moral and physical health of soldiers. In addition to the effects on the military, the sex trade during the Civil War also had lasting consequences for the women and men involved in the trade. Many of them likely contracted lifelong venereal diseases that resulted in sterility or even death. Other women became locked into the profession because of the "social stain" on their reputation. Cities associated with prostitution and general vice during the war also experimented with various approaches to those problems. Their efforts might have influenced other urban areas in the future because most large cities struggled with similar issues in the decades following the Civil War.

1

Morality and Prostitution in Antebellum America

During the Civil War, the terrible economic conditions for many women and the armies of young men away from families led to a huge increase in the population of prostitutes throughout the nation. The Civil War inspired the "largest increase in the sex trade in nineteenth-century America, perhaps the single greatest growth spurt in the nation's history."[1] Various officers in the Confederate and Union armies and civilian leaders viewed prostitution in different ways, with some choosing to ignore the situation and others attempting to eliminate visits to brothels completely. Still others, understanding the impossibility of keeping prostitutes and soldiers away from each other, made efforts to control the spread of venereal diseases. The views of officers and civilians on prostitution during the Civil War did not spontaneously form on the battlefields and in camps. They originated in the world in which these men came of age. Societal struggles over sexual knowledge and freedom that occurred during their youths shaped many officers' understanding of sexuality and its role in society. Just as prewar society influenced the men who went off to war, it also had a significant impact on the choices that were available to women during the war years. During the years leading

1

up to the war, upper- and middle-class society severely constrained occupations for women. Upper-class women usually concentrated their efforts in social or reform groups. Working-class occupations available to women largely consisted of expansions in the traditional female sphere: seamstress, cook, and domestic servant existed as the most prominent occupations for women. Though seen as "traditional" female occupations in the twenty-first century, antebellum society held the occupations of nurse and teacher as male-only positions. Women of the South experienced an even greater level of restriction on accepted gender roles. Urban women occasionally ventured into the public sphere to a limited degree by taking over their husband's business after his death, operating shops producing saddles or nets. Usually such women operated boarding houses, taverns, or worked in the needlework trade. Rural women largely remained confined to housewifery roles of selling eggs, butter, or milk, which was their only foray into the business world. African American women experienced an incredibly relegated existence in the South. Both slave and free African American women typically occupied the same roles in Southern society, working as domestic servants, serving as field laborers, and sporadically working as prostitutes.

Thirty years before the explosive growth of the prostitute population and efforts to control the trade during the Civil War, a struggle over sexual freedom and knowledge occurred in many of the major cities of the United States, such as New York City, New Orleans, Washington, D.C., and Nashville. During the 1830s and 1840s many people saw cities as centers of social menace.[2] This view arose from the changing circumstances of the movement of young, single men to America's population centers. Until the Industrial Revolution, most manufacturing occurred in small shops attached to the homes of craftsmen. The only employees in such establishments consisted of a craftsman, who might or might not own the building, and an apprentice or two. To the comfort of the apprentices' parents back home, the apprentices often lived with the craftsman and his family, with the craftsman looking after the apprentice as part of his own family. Similarly, many clerks in small retail shops and offices also lived in the households of their employers, with supervisors acting as surrogate father figures. This system proved fairly successful in keeping both clerks and apprentices from regular or frequent visits to what Victorian moralists regarded as morally bankrupt sections of the city. Like the domestic situation for apprentices, this arrangement put relatives at ease in the belief that an alternate parental figure safeguarded their sons.

Increased urbanization began to separate many small businesses from the dwellings frequently located at the rear of the establishment. On the whole, owners moved into residential areas and abandoned the use of the business districts as living space. With this change, the disappearance of the live-in apprenticeship soon followed. Just as the lodgings for apprentices dissipated, so too did the moral security of their adopted families.[3] As the business owners moved to residential locations away from their businesses, many clerks found shelter in boardinghouses where their employers usually could not supervise their leisure hours and provide a guiding hand.[4] Peer pressure served to push young men into outdoing their male comrades as continuing challenges to their masculinity. Many madams capitalized on peer pressure by hiring young men to befriend new arrivals to the city and lead them to particular brothels. Not wishing to appear less masculine or scared, the recent émigrés often accompanied their newfound friend to an evening of debauchery.[5] As a result of this lack of supervision and peer pressure, many of these clerks discovered means of entertainment that would meet with the approval of neither their families nor employers.

The lax oversight of the boardinghouse facilitated the ease with which young men could explore everything the city had to offer. Many boardinghouses lacked a final curfew when all residents had to be inside or suffer a night on the street after the proprietor locked the main door. The ability to come and go at any hour allowed, if not encouraged, youthful indiscretion to take hold and beckoned young men into patronizing late night establishments. The newly found freedom of the boardinghouse in itself likely seemed overwhelming to many new residents. Freedom, coupled with a willing guide in the form of a roommate or coworker, quickly introduced new arrivals to fresh forms of entertainment. Gambling on races, cards, fights, and blood sports, such as dog fights and bear baiting, became widely available. A plethora of alcohol, suggestive and explicit shows, and prostitutes could all easily be found in the confines of most US cities.[6] Many such diversions appeared in working-class neighborhoods, readily available and often located along the route home for many clerks. Another attraction consisted of the cheap food frequently sold in taverns. Low-cost cuisine almost certainly served as the lure to get clerks into taverns. The practicality of drinking alcohol also drew clerks to taverns. City water supplies emanating from cities' cisterns often became tainted with a plethora of bacteria, which resulted in potentially life-threatening diseases. Drinking and eating in taverns proved not only cost effective, but it also appealed to patrons as a healthy option. Although drinking alcohol and eating in taverns could certainly be innocuous, the gambling and prostitutes also present in the buildings were not. The more time patrons spent within the taverns, the more immured the young men became to such behavior.

The increasingly large numbers of young men leaving rural homes to find a form of professional work in the cities during this period exacerbated this problem. In addition to the shuffling of the previous apprentices to boardinghouses, droves of young men moved from rural settings under the supervision of their families to cities with more temptations and without the traditional safety net of an apprenticeship. In response to the threat to their sons' morality, many parents purchased one of the several advice books being published as a guide to maintaining the principles of young men in these "dins of iniquity."[7]

Advice guides covered a variety of subjects for young men entering the changing cities of the nineteenth century, from warning them about entrapments to advising them on sexual matters. Many of these guides represented sexual temptation as dangerous and sought to repress such feelings.[8] According to one guide, when a young man entered a city he should be aware of the many who would take advantage of him. Guides reported confidence men as taking interests in youths to entice them into amoral lives of vice, destroy their character, and place them in the service of the confidence men.[9] Although the guides offered a somewhat overdrawn interpretation of confidence men, merchants or brothels actually hired these men—known as drummers—to "drum up business." At times, brothels also employed young men to befriend new arrivals and be a form of advertising for a particular brothel.[10] Although it seems unlikely that many confidence men sought to employ youths in their own dishonest money-making schemes, for business reasons, many led them into sexual temptation through a trip to a brothel. Furthermore, merchants frequently had clerks take out-of-town clients to brothels as a means of creating loyal customers by "showing them a good time." Although young men might seek to avoid the sex trade, it often came looking for them in the form or drummers, peer pressure, or even entertaining a client from work. Through their actions of presenting women as commodities to be used and cast aside, drummers reinforced ideas of masculinity asserting males as the dominant sex. At best, the males adopted the image of the "Madonna and the whore," in which some women could be treated as sex objects whereas others should be respected and treated as proper ladies.[11]

Moralists feared the peer pressure that drummers as well as other young men residing at the boardinghouses had on their sons. Newly arrived young men desiring to create a sense of belonging among their peers often agreed more readily to follow other young men for a night out on the town as part of the attraction of city life. Popular nineteenth-century phrases such as "I have seen the elephant!" in letters and common usage denote the idea of journeying to a place and seeing all that it has to offer.[12] Although this phrase would resurface during the Civil War as a reference to witnessing a soldier's first combat experience, the phrase had a racier connotation in reference to a visit to the city, such as a visit to a brothel. Such letters to acquaintances reveal that young men not only faced peer pressure from their contemporaries in the boardinghouses, but also their bragging suggests that they felt these pressures from hometown friends as well.

According to the advice guides and preachers of the day, not only should confidence men be feared, but also "there is the hardened pander to vice who has as little remorse at the ruin of innocence as the alligator has in crushing the bones of the infant that is thrown into his jaws from the banks of the Ganges: and there is she—who was once the pride and hope of her parents—who now makes war upon virtue and exults in being a successful recruiting-officer of hell."[13] Although the confidence men or peers recruited young men into amoral entertainment, the city prostitutes formed the sexual pinnacle of fear for the reformers and families. Extreme examples such as this also hint at the lengths reformers would go to use horror and biblical references to scare young men into leading moral lives.

From moralist newspapers to advice guides, the gamut of sexual activities of young men received careful scrutiny. Not only did moralists warn men to avoid prostitutes, but they also considered masturbation a transgression. Doctors even counseled offenders that by cutting out "tea, coffee, meat, and sugar," the compulsions to act out would subside.[14] As proof of the widely held concern, doctors in several cities evidently specialized in quelling "nocturnal emissions."

Ironically, many of these warnings actually drew men to the cities, however, because they found the warnings a hint at the excitement that the city offered.[15] Many young boys left for the city with a copy of an advice guide in their pocket and promises to avoid questionable establishments, but all the while planning which of those locales to visit first. The generational disconnect of parents and their inability to confound the sex drives of young men nullified most of the efforts that parents, preachers, and other moralists hoped would distance these young men from corrupting influences.

Eventually, specialized publications fulfilled the adapted roles of advice guides for locating brothels for new arrivals. The emergence of urban "sporting guides" offers evidence of the attraction to cities for just such entertainment. Guides such as *The Whip*, *The Rake*, *The Flash*, and *The Libertine*, frequently distributed to newly arriving males at the depot or port, documented the locations of many nearby brothels as well as a review of the quality of their tenants. Whereas advice guides provided inspiration for some young men to journey into the city, sporting guides instructed them on *exactly* where to go when they arrived.[16] Drummers not only distributed sporting guides to clerks and other young men prior to the Civil War and then to soldiers in camps and cities, but they also circulated special editions for veterans at reunions in the years following the war.

For the most part, sporting guides referred young men to brothels housing the more expensive prostitutes. A great variety of locations for sexual commerce existed in nineteenth-century cities, and there was a vast continuum of situations for prostitutes. Many cities in the 1830s did not have laws against prostitution. Because prostitution either seemed inevitable or not a serious problem, prostitutes sought customers openly and sometimes even conducted business in the open. Women of several cities, including New Orleans, reportedly carried a scrap of rug on which to service clients after ducking into an alley or side street. Those cities that did have laws against prostitution ran the gamut from attempted abolition of the trade to a penalty system that allowed prostitutes and madams to conduct business in return for a periodic fine collected at the courthouse. These judgments to not see prostitution as a problem allowed the trade to continue in a wide variety of venues without serious fear of arrest. Prostitutes and their clients could still be arrested, however, on charges of disorderly conduct in areas where the sex trade was not illegal.[17] Similarly, the governments of several larger cities, such as Richmond and Memphis, realized the impossibility of stamping out the sex trade and chose to regulate the behavior of the prostitutes by fining them for unacceptable behavior.[18] Depending on the city, young men could find themselves in an area in which the sex trade was completely legal and open, a locale in which the trade was regulated as a means of maintaining order or supplementing town coffers, or areas in which the municipality attempted to totally abolish the institution. Later, during the Civil War, soldiers found themselves in the same circumstances with several cities and with officers who adjusted policies on prostitution as the situation demanded.

Although much sexual commerce occurred in brothels or other secluded locales, the theater existed as a large draw for sexual activity during the early nineteenth century. The reputation of the actress became sullied during this era because prostitutes often sought and serviced clients in the side boxes of the balcony and more famously within the third tier.[19] Theater managers admitted prostitutes for free or twenty-five cents, instead of the regular fare of one dollar, as a means of attracting male customers. Ladies of the evening could entertain only in the third-tier balcony, separated from the somewhat more refined theatergoers in the lower balconies. These areas proved safer than conducting business in an alley because the nearby crowds ensured witnesses should any difficulties occur. As a result, prostitutes frequented theaters with some attending several times a week.[20] This constantly available concession at theaters marked them as targets for reformers and for young men seeking the adventures of city life.

Nevertheless the plethora of brothels located in the cities provided the most obvious places in which to find sexual entertainment. During the 1820s, New York City had an estimated two hundred brothels—a number that grew exponentially with the increasing demands of unsupervised young men during the societal shift of the 1830s and 1840s. Most of these establishments concentrated in the tenant districts of Five Points, Water Street, and Corlear's Hook, which is a destination that may have inspired the term *hooker*. The women in these businesses charged between three and five dollars "at a time" in contrast to the usual dollar or fifty cent fare for a session with a streetwalker. This amount represented a substantial sum for an entry-level clerk who earned an average of four dollars per week. Unable to afford the high prices charged by brothel inmates, the lads probably sought out the company of the less-expensive streetwalkers in their neighborhoods. On the other hand, an experienced journeyman averaged ten to twelve dollars a week. Most brothel business probably originated from this better paid class of workers.[21]

Although room and board in a boardinghouse for a single clerk usually amounted to fifty cents per week, a prostitute's expenses could been considerably more. In the more exclusive brothels, which charged five dollars per visit, each tenant paid the madam an average of twelve dollars per week, a fee comparable to the contemporary rates of the elegant Astor House Hotel on Broadway with full meals included.

Despite this expense, select women of the more expensive houses saw around ten clients each week, a low number which was offset by their high rates. The lower number of clients also resulted from the amount of time the women spent with each customer. In addition to exchanging sex for money, higher-class brothels offered a number of services. The customer usually entered the establishment through a rather lavish parlor where he was offered a drink. Select businesses went so far as to hire cooks and build small kitchens to make full meals available for their clientele. Following the meal, a selection of cigars could be had, all the while enjoying the companionship of a suggestively clad young woman. If the fellow's money held out, he would then be led upstairs or to a back room by a Cyprian. With enough money, a sporting man could spend an "evening with Venus." More often, however, the time spent with "Venus" remained incredibly brief.[22]

As they got older, or the stress of the lifestyle hardened their once comely looks, prostitutes typically took a step down to that of conducting business in a small apartment, crib, or even becoming a streetwalker. By the time a woman made this move, the ambiance and seductiveness of Venus was gone and transactions took place with cold detachment. Out of desperation, streetwalkers occupied a wide array of habitations from abandoned buildings to back alleys, with others being completely homeless hoping that a client might provide shelter for the evening.[23]

Other women of the city turned to prostitution occasionally to make ends meet or to simply supplement their income. Women working in sweatshops of the early nineteenth century rarely made enough money to cover their necessities and many felt forced to turn to prostitution at times to survive. The temptation to prostitute proved incredibly strong. With most occupations closed to them, the only options usually open to women included laundress, seamstress, domestic servant, and prostitute. Seamstress ranked as the most prevalent position. Working usually seventy to eighty hours a week making shirts from morning until dark in a New York City factory, a seamstress typically earned one dollar. Room and board for an extremely economical place in the city cost around fifty cents a week at the time; with other needs such as clothing, medical attention, or supplemental food or drink, her expenses could easily creep dangerously close to her dollar wages and often exceed them. Any economic hiccup would bring about a serious budget deficit. A streetwalker, the bottom rung of status in the sex trade world, made the same amount of money for a single session with one client.[24] The ability to double her income for a few minutes work in a largely anonymous city when faced with dire economic circumstances might have been a tempting prospect.

Another avenue of sexual bargaining came in the form of treating. Young women went on dates with men, and in return for sexual favors, the male provided "gifts" of clothing or other valuables. Although women usually took part in occasional prostitution as a means of weathering a temporary economic shortfall, they typically used treating to obtain luxury goods that they might otherwise be unable to purchase. By looking at the transaction in the form of treating, neither party technically engaged in prostitution and could move on with the notion that their morality remained more or less intact.[25]

With the opening of the Civil War, desperation forced more and more women to find work outside of the home. Without their husbands or fathers to provide wage labor for the family while depending on irregular visits from the military paymaster, women faced economic pressures that increasingly burdened them, especially those with families. Lacking a stable income, more and more women ventured into the local economies as seamstresses, laundresses, or cooks. Eventually, the numbers of women seeking employment overburdened the local economies. The surplus female labor entering in the marketplace also forced down wages for the scant work available, which forced even more women to turn to prostitution as a means of survival.

Although sex workers as a whole rarely faced the more dangerous aspects of prostitution, some did become victims of the violence that often accompanied that world. Two famous murders of prostitutes sparked a radical change in the world of prostitution. A jealous client killed Helen Jewett, a high-priced brothel worker, and Mary Rogers, an occasional prostitute, was found dead in the Hudson River. The misfortunes of these two women became headlines in the emerging penny press that sensationalized their stories and created a frenzy in a successful bid to sell newspapers.[26] The rarity of a "deliberate murder" in New York helped sensationalize the events; at the time of Jewett's murder in 1835 there had been only seven recorded homicides in New York City.[27] As a result, subscriptions for newspapers of the penny press skyrocketed. Eventually, the more traditional newspapers (with their usual coverage of politics and economics) relented their formality and began to document the murders in light of the increasing penny press subscriptions.[28]

The newspapers sympathetically portrayed both Jewett and Rogers as having been victims of circumstances beyond their control. Editors reported that a suitor had taken advantage of Jewett sexually, which forced her to flee in shame to a life of prostitution as a fallen woman.[29] By reporting the story in this way, the press maintained Jewett's status as to uphold public interest in finding her killer. In an unintended effect, such reporting lured members of the middle class into the camps of several reform movements. Until this documentation by the newspapers, most of society ignored reformers that targeted prostitution and sexuality. The portrayal of the murders of Jewett and Rogers gave prudish Victorian society an excuse to discuss sexuality and morality in the growing cities. As a result, groups supporting the suppression of sexual knowledge that claimed it corrupted morality, as well as groups supporting the expansion of such knowledge, grew into powerful combative entities.[30]

Initially, the press portrayed prostitutes as victims of shameful circumstances under the control of tyrannical madams or unscrupulous theater owners in cities. Editors of sporting guides shot back, however, by praising the virtues of these beautiful young women full of character and kindness. That position likely reflected bias because these editors often had received preferential treatment.[31] Though these two interpretations of the circumstances appear too simplistic to describe the estimated six thousand brothel workers of New York in the 1830s, this materializing argument raised questions about the extent of sexual knowledge and women's power over their own bodies.[32]

One of the more significant and lasting responses to the sensational newspaper coverage of the Jewett and Rogers murders became the formation of reform groups specifically targeting the sex trade. In 1831, John R. McDowell took it upon himself to study the problem firsthand. McDowell had been a longtime promoter of reform. Several years before, McDowell published a newspaper known as *McDowell's Journal* as an agent of change. After several years, the *Advocate of Moral Reform* took over *McDowell's Journal* and by 1837 had more than 16,500 subscribers. The *Advocate of Moral Reform* argued that no help existed for women that had become prostitutes. The editors argued that once women started down that debaucherous road, there was no turning back, and often, they argued, the prostitutes did not want help.[33] Following his general efforts at reform through the newspaper media, McDowell focused on the sex trade. He claimed that men seduced virgins, forcing the young women into a life of prostitution as "soiled" women because no one would want to marry them. He argued that the women, however, "take their revenge an hundred fold," by seducing young male clerks and apprentices in the city.[34] In what he would term, *The Magdalen Report*, McDowell claimed that nearly two hundred brothels and numerous tenements housed prostitutes.[35] In a curious move, *The Magdalen Report* also provided the names and addresses of many of the aforementioned brothels.[36] Like the advice guides, this information undoubtedly frightened parents and enticed young men. Understanding that most prostitutes did not reside in brothels, but instead worked as dance hall girls, crib women, and streetwalkers, McDowell endeavored to enumerate all of the prostitutes residing in New York. After careful study, McDowell arrived at the considerably inflated figure of ten thousand prostitutes. Although McDowell worked in the poorer areas of the city promoting a reform agenda, he had a basis for his estimate. As a member of the New York Tract Society, a Christian group that distributed religious pamphlets, however, McDowell's results are questionable. By largely exaggerating the number of prostitutes in the city, McDowell very likely sought to secure church backing to rescue prostitutes and garner new morally concerned members for churches.[37]

Detractors of *The Magdalen Report* also allowed their biases to influence their statistics. Chief among the detractors stood Tammany Hall. On August 20, 1831, members of Tammany Hall "passed resolutions demanding proof" of the numbers of prostitutes in the *Magdalen Report* and charged "that we will not rest until these base slanderers be punished." Tammany countered with a much lower estimate of 1,438 prostitutes. Like McDowell, members of Tammany Hall also worked with prostitutes, more often as clients, however, rather than as religious reformers.[38] Among their number, Daniel Edgar Sickles would go on to command a brigade during the Civil War. Sickles regularly consorted with prostitutes, going so far as to introduce a Cyprian named Fanny White to the Queen of England as the wife of Horace Greely. The two widely divergent estimates clearly reflect the biases of both parties. The actual number is believed to be closer to an average of the two figures, with prostitutes likely numbering nearly six thousand at the time.

Although a dialogue about sexual knowledge occurred among rural citizens, the population shift to urban centers brought about a change in the traditional networks among women. At this time, rural women relied on each other and the wisdom from older members of their networks for subtle advice on methods of birth control—both preventative and abortive. With the move to the city, these networks of advice lessened, which fostered the need for a new source of information. These new forms of advice came into print or in lectures, and as a result could be easily targeted by reformers. In "1829, Frances Wright and Robert Dale Owen opened the Hall of Science in New York City" with plans of creating similar institutions in other cities. As one of its missions, the Hall of Science taught about sexuality and distributed birth control information through lectures and pamphlets. The Hall became a surrogate for the rural network for sexual information. As news about the lectures spread, more and more New Yorkers began to visit the Hall. Eventually, the lines for the lectures stretched around the block.[39]

Curiously, Wright and Owen located the Hall of Science directly across the street from the New York Tract Society. The Tract Society sought to start the conversion process of New Yorkers through the use of religious print. To members of the Tract Society, the location of the Hall of Science provided a clear sign of the morally bankrupt state of the city. A close affiliate of the Tract Society, McDowell even charged that Wright and Owen conspired with Tammany Hall. Possibly in retaliation, someone printed "various obscene pictures" of McDowell.[40] The proximity of these two opposing societies portended the exciting battles that would follow. The tractarians opposed birth control as dangerous because it "removed the fear of pregnancy, believed to be necessary for the protection of female virginity."[41] If such knowledge became widely distributed, they believed that sexual morality would disappear and society would fall into chaos.

In response to the location of the Hall of Science and its popular lectures, the tractarians began producing cheap tracts to give away to people standing in line outside of the Hall of Science. Initially the opposing freethinkers sold books promoting their ideas, but these books were too expensive for the general public. Eventually, they responded by printing their own "tracts." An "explosion of print" followed, with agents of each society distributing tracts in the street between the two establishments to crowds gathered there.

Wright argued that a relaxation of standards did not create the current moral questions being addressed in the city. She stated that the climate of sexual repression fostered such problems. According to Wright, if the natural passions were not expressed, they would become distorted and "women become prostitutes or prudes and men, rakes."[42] She also believed that if women became fully aware of her teachings, the power of men over women would dissolve. Richard Carlile's *Every Woman's Book* went further by stating that women "must satisfy their sexual needs or turn sour . . . their physical form degenerates, they become fidgety and suffer from melancholia and consumption, turning into what the world recognizes as old maids."[43] Furthermore, Owen claimed that masturbation led to insanity. He saw a way to curb such urges by the distribution of birth control means. With such knowledge couples could engage in sex with less concern about pregnancy.[44] Wright, Owen, and other freethinkers used such teachings to rationalize the world of sexuality, although some of their interpretations were as outlandish as the moralist side during this period of limited medical knowledge.

Opposition groups condemned Carlile's teachings as granting "inducements and facilities for the prostitution of their daughters, sisters and wives."[45] A popular leader of the religious moralists, the Reverend Lyman Beecher, referred to their past experiences in utopian and free-love communities, and he charged that Owen and Wright intended to "abolish private property, put children in state nurseries, and destroy the family." Beecher also argued that they promoted atheism and the "temptations of the Devil," such as sexual gratification, through their lectures and printed material at the Hall of Science.[46] Through their use of biblical themes, religious groups attempted to halt the dissemination of knowledge by groups like the Hall of Science. Or at the very least, the moralists attempted to reform people already living in what they deemed as hedonistic lifestyles to maintain the ideals of Victorian America.

As conversion of the alleged "immoral" elements of the city became increasingly unlikely, one group formed in an effort to safeguard the moral fiber of its members. In 1852 a group of Christian businessmen joined together to establish a chapter of the Young Men's Christian Association (YMCA) in New York City. They hoped to "offer safe havens for 'moral' recreation to young clerks surrounded by temptation."[47] In addition to providing morally sound companionship to young men, the YMCA had other benefits, one of which was entering an established business network.[48] As a means of seeking employment, it is highly likely that some new arrivals took advantage of the easily accessible business contacts offered by the YMCA simply as a means of procuring employment while misleading the group in terms of their devotion to Christianity. Evidence of this practice can be seen during the Panic of 1857, when membership in the organization jumped to sixteen hundred.[49] Although prostitution and crime probably increased during the Panic simply as a result of economic pressures, the new members of the YMCA in all probability joined for the benefits that the group offered. The YMCA offered dormitory type structures, reasonably priced meals, and the possibility of meeting acquaintances that might

The YMCA in New York City provided a place for moral young men to congregate within the city. During the war, some soldiers likewise congregated under the YMCA banner as a means to safeguard the morals of the group.

help members weather the storm of the Panic. Members of the YMCA almost certainly knew that some recruits joined for reasons other than moral security, but the devout within the group likely saw the issue as the potential to convert the nonbelievers or bring the lax closer to the Christian God.

With the beginning of the Civil War in 1861, the YMCA found a natural place among citizens seeking to support the war effort. Rather than endeavoring to save city clerks from "moral bankruptcy," members shifted to "saving the Northern soldiers from their own moral weaknesses."[50] With sound logic, members agreed that soldiers away from the security of home for the first time faced a situation similar to the young men entering the cities seeking employment. Alcohol, gambling, and prostitutes held as much, if not more, sway in army camps as they did in America's cities.

As both groups attempted to present their views to the public in the years before the Civil War, many of their subscribers became more entrenched in their respective beliefs. This resulted in very little compromise or movement between the two groups. Most female freethinkers remained unlikely to concede the right of male authority over their lives and sexuality, especially with the emerging women's suffrage movement underway. Likewise, moralists did not publicly reveal any change in their views of sexuality. Any shifts in ideology received expression for the most part only to spouses while publicly maintaining the façade of a proper member of the community.

Some citizens, and later soldiers during the war, identified their feelings of masculinity in terms of morality and religion. They felt that their strong belief in God aided their ability to abstain from vice as well as remain brave during battle. Though some soldiers maintained such devotion, others found ways around their religion. Not all Christian soldiers equated their religious feelings to masculinity and morality. George Armstrong Custer possibly had at least one relationship with a prostitute; yet he wrote in a letter to his wife Elizabeth that his life remained "in the hands of the Almighty."[51]

Whether or not citizens of cities took up the argument on the morality of sexuality and the sex trade itself, the trade continued. Economic need remained the driving force behind the decision for most women to enter prostitution. Despite the efforts to retrain former prostitutes in trades such as sewing, laundry, or domestic work, the low pay for these professions limited successful reform. Alas, the debate over the sex trade never popularized the root cause of the issue and did little to reduce the population of prostitutes.

Though the cities of the North afforded women at least a debate on the issue of sexuality, the men and women of the South found their respective gender roles less fluid than those of the North. Southern gender roles evolved quite differently from those of Northern regions. In the Southern patriarchal society, males held legal control over most females—both black and white—in their lives. The slave system instilled an extensive level of control over the slave population and considerable control over their own families. Although most yeoman farmers did not own slaves, they subscribed to the strong gender roles of the South. Much of Southern society downplayed the lives of the elite women in the planter class. A widespread trend from the 1830s through the 1850s involved Southern editors promoting "anti-elitist [sic] rhetoric further by idealizing the busy farm wife as a more appropriate model of southern womanhood than the pampered, genteel lady of the aristocratic planter class."[52]

In the 1850s, Southern editors "began exhorting farm women to renew a supposedly weakened commitment to household duties." Editors blamed social aspirations and "selfish materialism for women's lack of attention to the home sphere and urged them to spend more time at home and to concern themselves less with worldly activities."[53] As women journeyed out of the household to become involved in social organizations or to obtain some education, they seemed to be slipping gradually from the control of the male population. By the middle 1850s, some Southern editors had begun downplaying such efforts as frivolous and encouraging women to revert to "traditional" roles as wives. In 1857, an edition of the North Carolina newspaper, the *Observer*, noted that housewives bore the cause of the climbing prices of some farm products. The paper claimed that these women "can play the piano, but cannot churn; can dance, but cannot skim milk; can talk a little French, but don't know how to work out buttermilk."[54] Some men even urged those few women who did seek out a formal education to keep their interests in the female realm. James A. Long addressed the Edgeworth Female Seminary in 1858. During his speech he admonished the graduating class to remain out of politics. He warned them against "soil[ing their] garments with matters which do not pertain to [their] position in society."[55]

Although some women sought education, most Southern women worked alongside their families attempting to contribute to the family's income or farm production. If they involved themselves with wage labor, Southern women, like Northern women, typically did not earn enough money to support themselves if a male was not a household earner as well. In cases of women-led households, several unmarried women might band together in a single home as a means of jointly supporting themselves. If such an arrangement did not manifest itself, single women took on any work that they could find to support themselves. Historian Victoria Bynum concluded that: "To avoid the county poorhouse, a dismal institution that did little more than warehouse the poor, some women worked long hours in the homes and fields of others and occasionally turned to prostitution, thieving, or illicit trading."[56] When the Civil War began, many women temporarily or permanently lost their male heads of households. More and more women found themselves in situations in which they needed to provide for their survival alone. The situation became worse when thousands of women experienced similar circumstances that drove down their already meager wages.

Divorcées usually became destitute prior to the war. Whether they left their husbands, or their husbands abandoned them, society viewed most divorcées as "ruined" or even "fallen" women.[57] Some divorced women avoided the stigma of being a divorcée and even married well. Rachel Robards Jackson, President Andrew Jackson's wife, and Peggy Eaton, wife of Secretary of War John Henry Eaton, are examples of antebellum divorcées who overcame that status. Society held a harsher view of most female divorcées, however. Madaline Selima Edwards divorced her first husband and attempted to survive on her own in antebellum New Orleans. According to her diary, she realized that the only men that she could then attract would be from the working class. Although Edwards came from a family of moderate means in Tennessee, she went to school until the age of fourteen.[58] Thus, she had more skills to offer than the typical single female in the South. She sold paintings, took sewing work, and even taught school. These trades did not provide enough income to support her fully.[59] Dell Upton, who edited Edwards' diary, concluded that although the young woman never admitted to earning money through prostitution, there are many hints she engaged in the sex trade throughout the diaries. In several situations, Edwards received money from various male friends. At other times she claimed they paid for her laundry, and on other occasions she begged them for some unnamed work.[60] Whether or not Edwards participated in the sex trade, her level of education and various occupational skills did not keep her from the lowest levels of poverty that often lured women into the trade.

The laws concerning prostitution in the South varied widely in their enforcement. Most larger communities enacted laws against prostitution; yet many courts merely attempted to curtail or restrict prostitution to certain areas of town rather than attempting to abolish the trade completely.[61] For the most part, authorities allowed prostitution to occur in Southern towns and cities as long as the trade complied with two basic guidelines. The women and their clients usually had to maintain a semblance of decency, not disrobing or flaunting their profession in public thoroughfares. Restrictions on the openness of the trade vastly differed among Southern cities. Some city governments attempted to tightly control districts in which the trade flourished, whereas other cities, such as New Orleans and Memphis, did little but allow the trade to flourish in close to a free-market situation. In addition to the loosely established "red light districts," prostitutes also contended with a racial double standard. As long as white prostitutes only catered to white men, and not African Americans, the courts did not charge the women with a crime. Bynum noted that: "Indictments for prostitution particularly targeted women who engaged in interracial social activity or who operated taverns at which blacks and whites were suspected of gambling, drinking, and exchanging illegal goods. Prostitution was usually included within the general charge of operating a 'disorderly house,' rather than being the sole issue of an indictment."[62] Conversely, white males saw African American prostitutes and kept free and enslaved mistresses with little fear of societal judgment or criminal indictment. The white male maintained this social discretion by abstaining from escorting the lady to social gatherings and treating her only as a mistress.[63] Unlike white prostitutes, African American prostitutes held the capability of catering to either race without repercussions. Unfortunately for African American women, if a male attacked, robbed, or raped them, they could not file charges in a court of law because they could not testify against whites in court.

In addition to financial hardship, some women of the South faced a precarious existence on the edge of respectability. Though white men slept with African American women and faced little if any repercussions, a white woman who crossed the racial line would be shunned in middle- and upper-class society, leaving little opportunity for redemption. Society likewise shunned most female divorcées, leaving them only the choice of a second husband from the ranks of lower-class males.

Much of society regarded cities of the 1830s and 1840s as centers of social menace and immorality. Rapid urbanization, the transition of the industrial revolution, the anonymity of city life, and the great availability of vice combined to cause great concern. Young men ventured to American urban centers in the hopes of "seeing the elephant," while being countered by advice guides, the efforts of the YMCA, and other moralist groups. Likewise, many young women alone in the cities found it difficult to earn a living and turned to prostitution. The sex trade paid much more than traditional occupations available to women of the period. Newspaper editors frequently capitalized on the scandalous nature of prostitution and used titillating items to sell papers. Such reports, in turn, fueled the moralist crusades to eradicate prostitution and other forms of vice. One of the most famous reform groups identified itself as the Magdalen Society. The society overestimated numbers of prostitutes in New York City in an attempt to motivate citizens into action. Their numbers, however, faced a much lower counter estimate from the corrupt forces of Tammany Hall. Another group in opposition to the moralists established the Hall of Science to hold lectures on sexuality and birth control. Opponents argued that the group sought to take away fears of pregnancy and disease with the information, which ultimately harmed the morals of society.

Southerners did not engage in the same degree of debate on sexuality and gender roles. Although gender roles did not remain completely static during the antebellum period, they did not have the same degree of flexibility as those in the North. Newspaper editors as well as larger society worked to restrain Southern women within their traditional roles. Such conditions, however, did not prepare them for an easy transition to financial independence during the war. In light of these adversities, many women, especially in the South, turned to prostitution for survival during the Civil War. Although Southern cities varied their enforcement of laws against prostitution, most typically adhered to a policy of controlling the trade with a focus on maintaining the peace.

The ingraining of conflicting beliefs concerning sexuality and prostitution in the young soldiers of the Civil War, as well as the reinforcement of beliefs of older officers, played out during the early years of the war with attempts to regulate the morality of camp life or to allow permissive environments that flourished in other camps. Although the camps of generals such as Daniel Sickles and Joseph Hooker reflected the stereotypic ideas of a hedonistic camp life, reformers such as the YMCA and the Christian Commission transferred their attempts at controlling the sexuality and morality of the cities to the camps of young men away from familial supervision.

2
Women in the Sex Trade

When most people in the mid-nineteenth century thought of women who sold sex, various callous synonyms for the trade usually came to mind: harlot, hooker, whore, strumpet, women of ill repute, and even "agents of Satan," as Lyman Beecher occasionally referred to them. Such period monikers did little to capture the complete nature of the sex trade.[1] Likewise, more innocuous synonyms such as ladies of the evening, soiled doves, dutch gals, Cyprians, daughters of Eve, and gay young ducks did not provide accurate descriptors either. Although the first group of euphemisms clearly held the women morally accountable for their employment situation, the latter group seemed to suggest that prostitution as a career involved women whose circumstances inadvertently led them to the lifestyle—soiled doves—or that they adopted the career almost as a lark—dutch gals. Unfortunately, almost no title for prostitutes failed to carry with it a negative or almost whimsical connotation. Even the word *prostitute* had a gritty, almost polluted feel.[2] Although "women who worked in the sex trade" would be a more accurate description, such women will be referred to primarily as prostitutes for the sake of brevity.

This chapter explains the circumstances surrounding a woman entering the sex trade and shows that women exercised some authority over their lives instead of the usual portrayals of prostitutes as passive actors and morally bankrupt people. The vast majority of prostitutes worked as streetwalkers who sought a means of survival and barely earned a living. A smaller number became brothel workers and earned an impressive living during a time in which women were limited in career choices.

Some women chose prostitution as a means of earning an income during the war years because those who chose other paths of employment had fairly limited options. Society largely restricted female occupations to "traditional" roles such as seamstresses, laundresses, or domestics. The region in which the women lived during the war also affected the available options. As a more industrialized region, the North offered women more opportunity for employment, which increased when men went off to war in large numbers. This shift became acceptable because members of Northern society did not restrict the roles of women in their communities to the same extent as their Southern counterparts. As a strong patriarchal society, Southerners discouraged many female members from seeking an education or even working outside of the home.[3] An example of this is the school attendance rates for women in both regions. Around 70 percent of "school-age white girls" attended various schools in New England. In the South, only 35 percent of white girls attended school.[4] According to Reverend Francis Springer, a chaplain with the Union Army, "not more than one third, I am sure from actual count, were able to write their own name. Of the women, seven-eighths could not use the pen."[5] Although this may have been true for the small number of women that Springer talked with, Southern women as a whole did not exhibit overly striking differences in literacy than their Northern sisters. According to historians William J. Cooper, Jr. and Thomas E. Terrill, literacy among white Southern women "ranged from a high of 86 percent in Mississippi to a low of 64 percent in North Carolina." Women in the Northern states averaged a 90 percent literacy rate.[6] As young Southern men left for war, clerking in a mercantile did not provide an option for many Southern women. Shaped by culture or class, some upper-class Southern women subscribed to the status that Southern society created for them. This notion is reflected in a quote from Marcia Mason Tabb Hubard. On her forty-eighth birthday, her husband William cast his eighth cannon for the Confederate government and named it after Marcia. She wrote: "Most sincerely I do trust it will be a perfect one in every respect, and give more satisfaction and be of greater use than I have been in my worthless life."[7] Though surely most Southern women did not go to that extreme in their descriptions of themselves, her words offer a glimpse of the strong paternalistic sentiment in the South. White women did contribute to household chores and most definitely cooked, cleaned, and sewed in households without slaves or without slaves in sufficient numbers to accomplish such tasks. Many upper-class, slave-owning Southerners believed white women should be protected and sheltered from the harsh realities of life. Males or females who stepped outside of the accepted social norms quickly brought scorn on themselves. Pat Donnelly experienced such ridicule in April 1861 after whipping his wife. The *Memphis Daily Appeal* gaily claimed that the city recorder "charged Pat twenty-five dollars for his chivalric act. What a shame that was!"[8]

Such a characterization is precarious though. Although Southern society urged women to remain in accepted female roles of domesticity, the economic reality among many Southern families did not allow for such restrictions on female labor. The upper-class elite were the few people in the South able to maintain the state of perceived leisure among plantation mistresses. Even this is an illusion, however, because many plantation mistresses found themselves as constantly busy managers of the house slaves. Nevertheless, many Southern women emulated elites and sought to culture themselves through learning music or foreign languages. Some newspaper editors saw such activities as frivolous. In 1857, an edition of the North Carolina newspaper *Observer* "blamed the rising price of butter on housewives who 'can play the piano, but cannot churn; can dance, but cannot skim milk; can talk a little French, but don't know how to work out buttermilk."[9] Other North Carolina editors quickly picked up on the theme and "extended their antielitist rhetoric further by idealizing the busy farm wife as a more appropriate model of southern womanhood than the pampered, genteel lady of the aristocratic planter class."[10] Editors and other Southerners alike felt that too many women embraced the trappings of elitism and materialism rather than focusing on the daily tasks at hand. Such statements came to light during a backlash against a trend before the 1830s of Southern women stepping outside of their prescribed roles. More and more women became involved in social work outside of the household, in addition to cultural refinement. Women busied themselves with temperance societies, manumission groups—although these quickly focused on more humane treatment of slaves than on freedom—and a few forays into governmental business.[11] From 1830 through the 1850s, Southern men attempted to halt the transformation of Southern women and guide them back into the traditional women's sphere. At times various Southern men made their goal blatantly apparent. James A. Long gave an address to the Edgeworth Female Seminary in 1858. During his speech, he admonished the young women against entering the political arena by warning them that they would "soil [their] garments with matters which do not pertain to [their] position in society."[12]

The women of Petersburg, Virginia, experienced similar restrictions on their roles in society. For the most part, the community accepted women working outside of the home in domestic-oriented businesses such as taverns or boarding houses. A few women in the city owned stereotypically masculine businesses—saddle making for example— but these women often inherited the business from a husband or father, which allowed for a social exception.[13] Although the husbands of married women attended to matters in court as legal heads of households, widows and single women of Petersburg, and much of the South, enjoyed a similar degree of access to the court system. Courts grudgingly had to accept increasing numbers of women involved in the legal system, especially in Petersburg where 33 percent of women lived as widows or bachelorettes.[14]

The paternalistic and largely rural Southern society served to limit women's chances once the war began. In the rural South, women working on small, slaveless farms "retained traditional roles in farming and household production: they spun, wove, sewed, made lard, kept gardens, fed poultry, and hoed corn."[15] Although these skills served the family to an important extent, many working-class women possessed such skills, reducing their value through competition on the open market. To keep women in such restricted roles, Southern "sermons, speeches, and periodicals [stressed] piety, innocence, submissiveness, intuition, compassion, and self-abnegation."[16] The constrained gender roles of women in the South directly stemmed from the pro-slavery defense of the region. Southern white men viewed themselves as the shepherds protecting their "property"—their family, slaves, and other belongings—from outside threats, as well as looking after the emotional and spiritual well-being of the people. Men occupied the role of a dominant and controlling father figure in Southern society. Most prostitutes did not originate from the slaveholding class, but the tradition of the husband as "master and protector" of his family and property existed for most Southern males. Although most working-class women probably did not have opportunities to better their financial situation by obtaining skills that might have made them a more marketable commodity anyway, it is unlikely that their husbands would have been open-minded or progressive enough to enable such a move. Southern masculinity, although varying in actual practice, translated readily across class lines. Wealthy males from the planter classes and other larger slaveholders figuratively placed their wives on pedestals, and placed them in charge of managing the house slaves at most, in an attempt to maintain a sense of Southern aristocracy. Southern families on small farms primarily could not afford such formalities, but the women of these families worked within the traditional women's sphere engaging in housework, gathering eggs, making butter, and mending or making clothing.[17] At planting and harvest time, the women helped in the fields.

In addition to the paternal restrictions on women during the antebellum period, the South did not undergo the "middle-class revolution that transformed northern society."[18] Although many women in the North expanded their roles outside of the home, most Southern women only saw such gains during the Civil War. The demands of the war mandated that women step outside of the accepted women's sphere. Working-class women quickly moved into factories and home industries. Most believed this to be only a passing state and that roles would return to normal when the war ended. Many women became contractors for the Confederate Quartermaster Department, making shirts and underwear among other fabric goods. The Quartermaster paid a scant "thirty cents a shirt and a quarter for underwear." The low wages had to be raised in Richmond in 1864 to "two dollars and a dollar, respectively" in light of runaway inflation exhibited in the Confederate capital.[19] Besides prostitution, several other fresh occupations for working-class women in the South opened up during the war years. One of those became positions in one of the gunpowder factories. As evidenced by period newspaper accounts, the likelihood of being blown up working in one of these factories proved almost as likely as catching a deadly venereal disease. Regular newspaper reports documented an average of twelve deaths from each explosion. As a means of curbing fears about working in such factories, the *Richmond Daily Whig* occasionally attested to the safety of a particular factory. On July 22, 1861, the editor claimed that nearly 370 women and girls made cartridges at the Thomas Factory with "no fear of accident." Yet the story directly above on the same page reported injuries in a factory from an "explosion of fulminating powder."[20] Another avenue for women opened as male teachers left to join the military. Although females only made up 7 percent of teachers in North Carolina before the war, they achieved parity during the war years. Historian Drew Faust stated that Southern presses sold the transition of women into the occupation by pointing to the dwindling numbers of males available and that the position suited females because of their "traditional maternal responsibilities as nurturers and instructors of their own young." Nursing also evolved into an occupation for Southern women. Originally reserved for elite women, the demands of war opened the field for working-class women who comforted and cared for wounded and sick soldiers.[21]

Similarly, Northern women experienced greater opportunities during the war. Because they did not face frequent invasions or the need to become refugees often, the newly vacated jobs left by soldiers in addition to the stereotypic female oriented jobs paid better than their Southern counterparts. Immigration continued in the North; however, the increased numbers beyond the norm did not alter the labor pool of most Northern cities. Marauding armies did not upset the routine of life in most Northern communities. During the war, Union women became teachers, nurses, clerks for merchants and the US government and agents for both the US Sanitary Commission and Christian Commission.[22] Furthermore, the war frequently had positive impacts on Northern cities. Whereas Richmond, Charleston, and some other Southern cities overflowed with refugees, suffered food shortages, and endured colossal inflation, larger cities in the North actually profited from the war.[23] The income generated from supplying the military with arms and supplies provided surplus money to the public.[24] According to the editor of the *Daily Morning Chronicle* (Washington, D.C.), the influx of money into Philadelphia alone had far-reaching effects. Crime was down, and masses of workers built more buildings during the war years than any time previous and laid miles of gas and water mains.[25]

Although several Northern cities, especially those with concentrations of soldiers, had problems with prostitution, the availability of other options for women, the boon economy, and a more reasonable rate of inflation made the growth of the sex trade much slower in the Northern states during the war. Like the prostitutes in the South, Northern women sometimes turned to prostitution as a means of survival or because of the lure of "easy money." Yet, the circumstances in the North allowed most women to avoid making this choice.

During the war, Southern cities saw tremendous numbers of refugees arriving daily. They arrived for a variety of reasons: Union forces approached or occupied their previous homes. Some families could not support themselves on small farms because of husbands or brothers away at war. On occasion, starving Confederate forces stripped a farm of food and left the residents hungry.[26] Whatever their reasons for coming, refugees arrived in droves. The sheer numbers of refuges strained the local economies. Previously meager food supplies became even more scant. Housing developed into a serious problem. Many of the refugees had no homes and the poverty that accompanied being homeless further detracted from their already low status among the cities' permanent residents. Surplus labor drove down the already low working-class wages, especially for women workers.[27]

With a plethora of fighting occurring within Virginia, the Confederate capital of Richmond endured an inordinate number of refugees that strained the city's resources. As the war drug on and circumstances worsened, the *Richmond Daily Whig* reported the plights of the refugees on a near daily basis. The paper claimed that a lot of worthy refugees in Richmond were starving. They had been "driven from lavish homes . . . to toil like slaves" and needed help from the local citizens.[28] Refugees required assistance primarily because of the skyrocketing inflation occurring in Richmond markets. The paper reported that eggs reached five dollars a dozen, butter was fifteen dollars a pound, beef was six dollars a pound, and flour had reached the astonishing price of two hundred dollars a barrel.[29] In addition to the inflation, refugees arrived with very few resources. Periodically, new arrivals sold off the furniture that they were able to bring with them. Although this generated some initial funds, the economic climate of the city soon demanded more.[30] In an article titled "Aid for Soldiers' Families," the writers of the *Whig* called on the permanent residents of Richmond to provide help, and although they did so in the first year of the war, it quickly became evident that everyone in Richmond was suffering and had to look largely to their own needs.[31]

As early as July 1861, Richmond began to experience food shortages.[32] Unfortunately, as conditions grew progressively worse, the residents of Richmond simply did not have enough to sustain themselves, much less enough to give to charity. The example of the family of General Albert Sidney Johnston captures the magnitude of the situation for Richmond and some other Southern cities. Following his death at the battle of Shiloh in 1862, Johnston's widow Eliza and their children had to provide for themselves. Although Johnston apparently possessed considerable wealth before the war, the family's circumstances had changed dramatically only a year after the general's death. In July 1863, General Gideon Pillow issued a call for aid for the family in the *Daily Richmond Whig*. Pillow claimed that the family was in "distress and destitution."[33] Although it is highly unlikely that Eliza ever resorted to prostitution to feed herself and family, the fact that the family of one of the highest-ranking Confederate generals required assistance should make one pause to consider the circumstances of the impoverished within the Confederate States. With little hope of receiving any sort of charity and few jobs available to them, most working-class women saw prostitution as one of their few options.

As women moved into the sex trade, they encountered a social and economic ladder within the profession. According to Anne Butler, prostitutes in the postwar US West ranged in age from fifteen to thirty.[34] Richmond exhibited the same age range during the Civil War. "Nearly 70 percent of the Richmond women in 1860 were between the ages of sixteen and twenty-four."[35] Though some women continued beyond the age of thirty, the entrance of younger women tended to push most older workers out of the business. During the Civil War, however, the upper age probably ranged somewhat higher. Western prostitutes usually catered to relatively small garrisons of frontier towns. Sex workers during the war catered to busy training areas and huge garrisons—such as the thirty thousand Union soldiers stationed in Nashville.[36] Age proved important in sex work. Younger, fresher faces usually could demand more money for their services. Younger women typically resided in brothels where the earning potential and economic liabilities were highest. As brothel workers got older or the strain of the lifestyle began to show, they usually descended into one of the other three general categories for sex workers: saloon and dance hall girls, crib women, and streetwalkers. Saloon and dance hall girls worked in the saloons serving drinks, dancing, and seeing clients for sex on the side. Crib women stood one step above the streetwalkers. Women who no longer could pay "house fees" to saloon operators sometimes rented tiny one-room shacks and saw clients there. When their earnings no longer allowed them to afford the modest rent of a crib, prostitutes walked the streets and catered to clients on scraps of carpet or possibly in a room provided by the client with the hopes of spending a rare night indoors.[37] The theater remained a popular place to seek out most classes of prostitutes with the third tier of the establishment being understood as the area of the theater to find sex workers.[38] Among the masses of female streetwalkers, walked an extremely small number of male prostitutes. Such men occasionally dressed as women, which leads to the clear assumption that male prostitutes catered to male soldiers during the war.[39] Unfortunately, as sources on female prostitutes remain somewhat elusive, documentation of male prostitutes is almost completely absent with only a handful of sources mentioning their existence.

The desperation of starving women, coupled with the libidos, cash, and freedom of soldiers away from home, led to a tremendous boom in the sex trade market. Anywhere that Northern armies trained or assembled for any length of time, prostitutes quickly descended on the area.[40] Most assuredly, the same can be said of Southern armies. The governments of both capital cities—Washington, D.C., and Richmond, Virginia—enacted laws attempting to control the soldiers assembled there. Authorities in both capitals tried to prohibit soldiers from acquiring alcohol and engaged in half-hearted attempts to keep soldiers from visiting prostitutes. Both programs quickly proved impractical. Placing prostitutes into jails became completely infeasible. Richmond mainly used its jails to house prisoners of war, spies, and other serious criminals. Washington, on the other hand, used the district penitentiary to store ammunition; with both the county jail and workhouses being easily escaped.[41]

Realizing the impossibility of confining all of the prostitutes, authorities attempted to control the sex trade as best as they could. The Mayor's Court in Richmond typically charged sex workers a "security for their good behavior" of two hundred dollars and then released them.[42] Though the "fine" for keeping a house of prostitution in Richmond was two hundred dollars, the fine for selling alcohol to soldiers was twenty dollars. This disparity makes the fines for madams sound suspiciously like a licensing fee in disguise. The courts of Washington chose a different route. Rather than charging "securities," authorities of the city simply tried to make the prostitutes behave. The *Daily Morning Chronicle* often printed reports of prostitutes getting arrested for bad behavior. In February 1863, the paper reported that police arrested eight women at Sarah Austin's brothel for "disorderly conduct." The court fined the women a mere $2.94 and released them. Apparently, the small fine was meant to serve as a warning. On the same day the paper stated that police broke up another brothel. The inmates reportedly became drunk and two were fighting. Evidently previous disturbances had occurred within this particular brothel because Superintendent William B. Webb took the keys to the house and would not allow for its further use as a brothel.[43]

The relationship between prostitutes and various government and military officials proved tense and often contradictory during the war years. Prostitutes often had a lukewarm relationship with local officials—both military and civilian. For the most part, locals tended to tolerate the sex trade because little could be done to stamp out the business completely. As long as women working as prostitutes behaved themselves by staying in their unofficially designated areas of town and did not flaunt their activities in public, local people and officials tried to ignore the issue. Much of the continuum of treatment can be seen in the Richmond newspapers. At times, the judge of the Mayor's Court treated prostitutes with contempt. For example, the *Richmond Whig* reported on July 12, 1861, that Peter Kennedy and Matt Kevan faced charges of threatening to "assault and shoot a Mrs. Mary Sullivan." Ultimately the mayor dismissed the charges, however, after an Officer Seal stated that Sullivan was "one of the most intractable and intolerable women in the city." According to the newspaper, both "parties returned to their shanties, near the head of the dock" after the hearing.[44] Although not stated by the editor, the mayor may have summed up the entire event as a common working-class conflict.

The mayor also heard the case of Mary Elizabeth Carrington on the same day. Although he ordered the young woman to serve two days in jail on a charge of "drunk and disorderly," the court evidently had been lenient on her previously. A month before, authorities arrested Mary "for hacking a soldier in the small of the back, with a hatchet . . . for offering some indignity."[45] The paper did not state why the city failed to charge Mary with attempted murder after her arrest or whether or not that she had already served time for the incident. Probably the city of Richmond did not have space to house any but the most serious offenders. After all, the city officials faced an ever-increasing tide of prisoners of war that required, at least temporary, housing in and around the city.

Five days later, on the 17th, the *Richmond Whig* printed an article concerning a brothel run by Lizzie Winn. The authorities charged Winn with "keeping a disorderly house of ill fame in Locust Alley." The mayor ordered her to pay a "$200 security for future good behavior, and informed her that the recognizance would be forfeited if she continued to keep the establishment. Moreover, he would send down a force of police to arrest every person found in the house."[46] The significance of the charge seems to lie in the "disorderly" component of the brothel. In other reports by the *Richmond Whig*, the mayor typically ordered prostitutes to pay the security with no warning of ending their work. In this case, however, the mayor seemed to be at the end of his patience with the antics occurring at this particular brothel and closed the establishment.[47]

Although the mayor attempted to keep the Cyprians and other "miscreants" under control through charging securities and short stints in jail, he also periodically took their side in legal matters when the law favored the prostitute. In 1864, the mayor sent a Union deserter named Bill Gantry to Castle Thunder for stealing some furniture from a local sex worker. Although Gantry's status as a Union deserter seems problematic appearing before a Confederate judge, at least occasionally, sex workers and other people on the bottom rungs of nineteenth-century society received a fair break.[48]

The mainstream press periodically praised the worthy actions of select prostitutes. The *Memphis Daily Appeal* reported in April 1861 that a prostitute named Susan Striker was murdered by Charles Burton. Apparently he shot Striker when she ordered Burton to stop abusing his wife. The editor of the paper, an outspoken critic of beating women, lauded Striker as a fallen noble woman. He concluded the story with the words: "God bless her memory."[49] Although the press frequently criticized prostitutes for attacking the moral standing of the community, on occasion editors saw the humanity at the core of these women.

Not only did women in urban areas sell sex, the rural women of the period practiced the trade as well. Although women in rural areas had a better chance of providing for themselves than their urban counterparts, rural women faced different challenges. When males enlisted into the Confederate military, they did not leave women helpless on farms, but an important source of labor in the fields had gone. Many farm families included several children. Older children often met the overwhelming labor demands of the farm. The lack of an older son, however, or a family with younger children unable to help with much of the work put the mother in dire straits. In such conditions, the wives of subsistence farmers had to try to raise and harvest crops, care for young children, prepare meals, mend clothes, attend to any livestock that the family may have owned, all the while living in fear of their husbands' death and invading Yankee armies.[50]

Work at home for women in the nineteenth century required considerable time. Food preparation provides a clear example. To cook one had to build a fire. As the fire reached a cooking temperature—if chicken was on the menu—the cook had to kill, clean, and butcher the bird. Women prepared a majority of the food at the time as single-pot meals, usually stews and roasts. Although the single-pot meal saved time, such meals likely took anywhere from three to four hours to prepare, depending on the time spent catching the chicken. With such extensive demands on women's labor during the war, it is understandable that many rural women became destitute.

When armies of either side drew near, rural women sometimes engaged in the sex trade as a means of staving off hunger. Unfortunately, some soldiers from both armies who ventured into areas with rural prostitutes only saw what they termed as "the lack of virtue" in the area. In October 1864, a Confederate private in rural Alabama wrote to his wife: "We are in the poorest pine country you ever saw, the people can raise nothing but potatoes. The state of morals is quite low as the soil. Almost all of the women are given to whoredom and [they are] the ugliest, tallow faced, shaggy headed, bare footed, dirty wenches you ever saw."[51] The year before, another Confederate soldier near Chattanooga reported: "The war appears to have demoralized everybody and the rumor says that almost half the women in the vicinity of the army, married and unmarried, are lost to all virtue."[52]

Understandably, many soldiers likely worried about the state of morality in their hometowns and among their families. Accounts by both soldiers and civilians from most areas of the Confederacy testify to the lack of virtue and hard-scrabble conditions. The words of a Confederate major can be applied to many places in the section: "Prostitutes are thickly crowded through mountain and valley in hamlet and city."[53]

The currency that soldiers used to purchase sexual services dismisses many of the charges of immorality among Southern women. Rather than cash, many prostitutes could be had in exchange for food. As federal troops approached civilian areas, they occasionally "pressured [destitute women] into prostitution by the offer of Federal provisions." An Atlanta woman claimed in a letter to her husband that federals offered her provisions in return for sex in September 1864. She claimed that although she did not accept the offer, several of her neighbors did. In return for sex, the neighbors received flour, meal, meat, sugar, crackers, and coffee.[54] Although this woman may have been telling the truth, her words remain suspect. Of course she would not want to either upset her husband while he was away at war or even worse admit to being unfaithful, no matter the reason. In addition to her relationship concerns, her resources must also be considered. With clear evidence that her neighbors exchanged sex for food, what prevented this woman from doing the same? Given their proximity to one another, it seems likely that she and the neighbors shared similar economic circumstances. If married, the other women probably also had husbands fighting in the Confederate military and possibly sending money home. Although financially strapped, the Confederate national and state governments found limited funds to aid the poor. Initially, only families of soldiers and sailors killed in service received such monies. Later, programs expanded to include all destitute people, although the available funds could not keep pace with demand.[55] Although governments made funds available, the Atlanta woman did not mention receiving any government assistance. Unless this particular woman had another source of income that allowed her to buy food—perhaps money her husband sent home—it is possible that she did partake in the exchange and misled her husband to spare his feelings and maintain her marriage.

Though her words require a degree of skepticism, the Atlanta woman may have been truthful. Just as there are possibilities that might have caused her to lie, there are various scenarios possible in which she told the truth. Strict religious or moral convictions might have prevented her from engaging in the sex trade. Furthermore, she may have had relatives that could help her through difficult times. Whether the woman received rations from federal troops, money from her husband or relatives, or subsisted on a starvation diet, historians can only speculate.

Quartermasters' warehouses could be a source of commodities such as foodstuffs, whiskey, coffee, or other supplies. Short on cash, both Confederate and Union soldiers took advantage of the food shortages facing civilians. Confederate soldiers repeatedly broke into the commissariat in Dalton, Georgia, "with a view of supporting these disreputable characters." Naturally, the flow of provisions attracted even more women willing to sell sex, to the point that an officer claimed the women were "impregnating this whole command."[56] Although such actions infuriated many of the officers, the trade satisfied the soldiers' desire for "companionship" as well as the hunger of starving civilians. Ultimately, several soldiers received courts-martial for misappropriating goods from the quartermaster.

Although some rural women occasionally prostituted themselves in return for provisions, other women actually followed the army as laundresses occasionally selling their bodies for extra income. Throughout US history, small groups of women followed the armies working as prostitutes. During the Civil War, as well as afterward, some women posed as laundresses while offering additional services as a prostitute.[57] Such an occupation could be doubly advantageous for women; not only did soldiers pay them to wash clothes, but the quartermaster also provided them with rations. Some women seem to have been "laundresses" in name alone, primarily occupying their time as prostitutes for the soldiers. The title of laundress allowed them to

Many destitute women sought employment with the armies as laundresses to support themselves during the war. Some of those women resorted to prostitution to further supplement their income.

collect rations as well as freely circulate among soldiers in camp—a right that many civilians did not have. Gradually the military restricted the freedoms of laundresses. In 1862, Confederate officers circulated an order to dismiss any laundresses not actually washing clothes.[58]

Although laundresses used their positions as a means of securing soldiers as clients, other women used their ability to pass as a male to travel as part of the army during their occasional forays into prostitution. One such woman journeyed to Nashville after selling her horse and saddle as a means of purchasing her fare. Writing to a friend back in Michigan, she described her adventure stating that once in Nashville she ordered the driver of an omnibus to "take me to one of the best fancy houses he knew so I stayed at 154 colledge [sic] street." The madam at the brothel charged thirty dollars in rent a week. She believed it a bit expensive but "supposed I could make it easy as any of the other girls and so I stayed there." She went on to say "Well I made money lots of it and lived in splendor. I made sometimes 75 dollars per day. You bet I dressed and rode in fine cariges [sic] and put on white (what do you think of that much) well I staied [sic] there about four months. I got tired and worred of that life so I began to study how to get out of it." She then donned male clothing, enlisted with a regiment from Michigan that was returning home, and left her temporary life in the sex trade.[59]

Soldiers during the Civil War had the *perceived* benefit of medical attention during the duration of their enlistment. They frequently sought medical help whether they contracted a venereal disease or some other malady. Although soldiers got fairly ineffective treatment, prostitutes had to pay for their medical care out of already precious funds. Because of their shaky economic circumstances, most prostitutes usually did not seek medical care in response to a venereal disease. Given the treatments for venereal diseases in the 1860s, however, often involving mercury or silver nitrate that doctors believed had the ability to kill an infection, the lack of money for medical care actually proved fortunate. Doctors usually administered doses of mercury as a means of staving off syphilis. Unfortunately, the mercury did nothing to cure the disease and probably made occurrences of dementia, which are sometimes caused by syphilis, even worse by adding other symptoms of mental impairment as a result of mercury poisoning. Physicians used silver nitrate in a urethral injection as a means of treating gonorrhea. This highly caustic solution caused a build up of scar tissue inside the urethra making urination increasingly difficult.[60] The effectiveness of silver nitrate was debatable.

When prostitutes infected with disease arrived in an area, they transmitted gonorrhea, syphilis, or the lesser-known disease orchitis to soldiers and some civilians. Those infected soldiers furthered the problem by infecting other prostitutes, who in turn infected more men. Therefore, the actions of many officers during the Civil War are understandable. For them, the most expedient way to end the epidemic seemed to be elimination of the prostitutes from the area. Without the prostitutes serving as carriers, most of the disease transmission would stop. Yet keeping soldiers completely away from prostitutes proved impossible with an estimated two thousand women selling sex to soldiers in Chicago, six to seven hundred more in Nashville selling sex, and untold numbers of prostitutes in other cities and towns.[61]

A terrible result of the sex trade during the Civil War became an epidemic of incurable venereal diseases. Although some diseases such as gonorrhea proved surprisingly treatable, the infection itself remained with the patients for the rest of their lives. Almost all of the people who contracted venereal diseases during the Civil War suffered with the disease for the duration of their lives and possibly passed the illness to other intimates such as wives and girlfriends because antibiotics were not widely available until the late 1940s.

In addition to probably enduring venereal diseases, prostitutes often had uneasy relationships with each other. Despite being described as "the lost sisterhood," the relationship between women in the sex trade often proved tenuous at best. Most prostitutes lived in severely limited economic conditions as well as being in direct competition with one another.[62] They could be amiable, however, when conditions allowed. Such conditions existed only when plentiful customers allowed all of the working women to make money. These situations usually occurred when garrisons occupied cities, or large armies moved through rural areas. In either circumstance, the throng of customers did not last long. When a garrison descended onto a city, very quickly outside prostitutes swelled the ranks of the local women thereby righting the supply and demand disparity. For a short time, the local women likely made a lot of money as the only providers of sexual services. Fairly quickly, however, "foreign" women arrived to ease the burden of the overworked locals and cash in on the bonanza. Although the new arrivals detracted from the overwhelming business that the locals experienced, the numbers of soldiers in the larger garrisons likely provided a passable income for all of those involved.[63]

The women of rural areas faced different situations. When armies moved though the countryside, the women who wished to sell sex only had a short period of time to do so. Because they mainly traveled by foot, the armies resembled huge snakes that twisted for miles on the narrow roads of the day. Rural women had the opportunity to make some money or trade for provisions over the next several days as the army passed and bedded down for the night. Some women sold baked goods to the soldiers, whereas poorer and starving women sometimes traded sex for any provisions that they could. Depending on how recently the particular army had been paid and how recently it had passed through other areas with women offering nearly identical goods, locals might make a short-term windfall from the passing army.[64]

Sex workers of the period should not be thought of as solely passive figures. Women had the power to unite and stage a massive protest if pushed too far or if their humanity was completely disregarded. Such an incident occurred in Richmond in 1863. The authorities made no apparent move to solve the case of a fellow sex worker who had been murdered at Alice Hardgroves's brothel. In an impressive show of solidarity, nearly three hundred prostitutes rallied at the coroner's office to protest the seemingly insincere efforts by the local authorities to find the killer.[65] Although the newspaper did not state the eventual outcome of the protest, the demonstration in itself speaks to the episodic solidarity and spirit that the women possessed. As reflected in less noticeable instances, prostitutes often defended themselves and other Cyprians from violence, appeared in the Mayor's Court in Richmond and other locations to lay claim to stolen property, and even violently retaliated if they felt wronged by the ill-mannered words of a soldier.

Occasionally at least, larger Confederate and Union forces contended over ladies of the evening. Following the battle of Nashville in December 1864, two prostitutes from Nashville journeyed to the location of the battlefield for a sightseeing jaunt. During their visit, they drifted to the western outskirts of the battlefield and to the outer reaches of Confederate patrols. Some Confederate cavalrymen captured the pair and, believing that they were spies, took them to Franklin and had them put under guard. After the Confederate Army of Tennessee disintegrated and abandoned Franklin to Union forces, several federals journeyed to the village and brought the ladies back to Nashville.[66]

A few months later in April 1865, Robert E. Lee surrendered his Army of Northern Virginia. Over the next several months, as the remaining armies of the Confederacy surrendered, many of the Union garrisons mustered out of the army. When their customers began the long-awaited journeys home, nearly all of the prostitutes catering to the armies did as well.

The end of the war did not improve the lots of many women. The Civil War resulted in the deaths of more than 600,000 soldiers. Many of these soldiers had wives back home that would have to carry on scratching out a living for themselves just as they had done for the last four years. These women were not incapable of supporting themselves and did not depend entirely on men to "save" them. Nothing could be further from the truth. Nineteenth-century US women had a remarkable knack for survival. Yet, the social norms established prior to the Civil War did create impediments for widows and unmarried women. Fortunately, the manpower shortages placed on the United States by the war opened some doors to women. The nursing profession came to include women during the war years, and it retained some of them during the postwar years. The war years also saw an increasing number of women in the teaching profession. The transition of the teaching profession into a female-dominated field became permanent, which granted many women lasting careers.

Such occupations could not support the tremendous numbers of single and widowed women in the postwar years. After the war, women clearly outnumbered men in several states. In 1870, women outnumbered men by thirty-six thousand in Georgia and by twenty-five thousand in North Carolina. In addition to a substantial number of white women seeking wage labor, nearly two million enslaved women gained freedom at the close of the war with almost half of them becoming wage laborers.[67] Although most white women did not compete directly for employment with African American women, those at the lower end of the class structure did.

For the most part, however, the avenue of selling sex for survival purposes closed for postwar women. Similar to the wartime situation, this occupational condition did not result from an increased sense of morality following the war. The demand for thousands and thousands of sex workers by the men of both armies simply no longer existed. At the conclusion of the war, the Confederate armies dissolved and the Union army shrank drastically in size. Although some demand existed for federal occupying forces during the Reconstruction years, far fewer federal soldiers remained in the South than there had been during the war years. As the Confederate soldiers and most of the Union armies mustered out of service in 1865, so too did the armies of working women who made the war a little more bearable for men far from home.

At its base, sex work during the Civil War focused on survival. Many women—Northern and Southern, urban and rural—found themselves in situations in which they had to depend on themselves as providers for their families. Social norms restricted roles for women and usually left women with very few options. During the war years, Northern women had slightly more avenues open to them: clerks in stores and others in addition to those offered to Southern women. Females living in the Southern states, however, faced a backlash against the movement toward more independent women in the early decades of the nineteenth century. Such a backlash did not maintain absolute authority though. To a degree, Southern society still allowed for women to work outside of the home, especially in more urban areas. Those positions often still did not pay enough to support completely a single woman. During the war, many women continued working on a farm or expanded domestic-related work, such as washing clothes or sewing. Many women found that with so many other women offering the same services, employers offered incredibly low wages. Others attempted to obtain work in industries in various cities. Openings in this field occurred at times and were often announced by a loud explosion at one of the munitions factories. As the war drained large numbers of men away from the larger cities, some women found work "in the War Department, the Post Office, the Quartermaster Department, and the office of the Commissary General" as clerks.[68] With more and more women competing for jobs during the war, some turned to prostitution as a means of survival. As refugees moved into Southern cities with roving armies, they unwittingly forced wages down. With the addition of runaway inflation, many Southerners faced precarious economic circumstances. In the first year of the war,

As the armies campaigned through the countryside, many civilians packed up as many of their belongings as they could carry and relocated to urban areas. Unfortunately, with so many refugees seeking employment to support themselves, wages plummeted and many women found themselves resorting to prostitution to survive.

aid societies formed in some cities to help the impoverished, but it soon became obvious that even people considered wealthy before the war had to struggle. The local working-class people and refuges had to fend for themselves with many becoming prostitutes. As numbers of prostitutes increased in Northern and Southern cities, local governments attempted to curtail the sex trade. As with so many other institutions during the war, they faced much more pressing issues. Eventually, most municipalities sought to control the sex trade, only arresting prostitutes if they caused trouble through physical attacks on others or general rowdiness. Rural women also sold sex; however, the bulk of their customers appeared sporadically in the forms of passing armies, leaving them little steady work in the trade.

Although women had the ability to provide for themselves and their families during the war, sometimes circumstances spiraled out of control, leaving them with the choice of engaging in prostitution or starving. Many prostituted themselves for money but also for the foodstuffs that proved to be the ultimate need. Unfortunately, by making this choice, they exposed themselves to venereal diseases that they would endure for the rest of their lives. As the war closed and men returned to civilian life, so, too, did most Civil War prostitutes. If for no other reason than the lack of a steady stream of customers, most prostitutes returned to a more normal life after the war. Larger towns and cities, however, still provided numerous clients for sex workers, which allowed prostitutes in those locales to continue in the trade, although their numbers fell to prewar levels. The fact that most prostitutes did not continue in the profession lends credence to the argument that most sex workers during the war years sold sex as a means of survival rather than simply having a supposed "immoral" nature.

3
The Soldiers

On 25 April 1861, Colonel Peter Turney gathered together his regiment of slightly more than one thousand men on the all-female campus of Mary Sharpe College in the rural town of Winchester, Tennessee. The men of the 1st Tennessee Infantry quickly readied themselves for a grand adventure. Each soldier gathered an inordinate amount of supplies for the war—most of which would be discarded during the first day of hard marching—and headed for the college. On the front lawn of the small campus, the young women of the college serenaded the men as they stood in their companies and an assembling crowd cheered the new soldiers.[1]

The women of the college represented the epitome of virtue, their morality safeguarded by an ever-watchful matron. The young men gathered on the grounds also likely remained inexperienced in the larger world of vice because most early volunteers came from middle- or upper-class families. Living in a relatively small town, most of the young men did not have an opportunity to engage in a great deal of misbehavior.[2] News traveled extremely fast among the people of nineteenth-century Franklin County, Tennessee. William Slatter, the editor of the local newspaper, *The Home Journal*, reported the local events of the middle- and upper-class community such as notable folks passing through town or even which neighbors called on who on Sunday afternoon. Furthermore any sort of scandalous news, although not reported by Slatter, crisscrossed the county even faster.[3] Therefore, not only did the parents of young men look to safeguard their morality, but the community at large did also.

As a result of the stern pressure to live a "moral and upright life," a sense of freedom washed over the men of the 1st Tennessee as they boarded a train on the afternoon of the 25th to Virginia. The same can be said of many of the young men that enlisted into Union and Confederate armies during the Civil War. For the first time in their lives, many of the men journeyed away from their home communities and the watchful eyes of parents, relatives, and neighbors. Not only would the men periodically move through large metropolitan areas for the first time in their lives, but they would also have the relative freedom to explore what these areas had to offer—well, as much freedom as their commanding officer would grant them.[4]

Although departing regiments left many of the home influences behind as they marched off under fluttering banners of glory, they retained more than they thought. The soldiers still received the occasional letter from home urging them to stay out of harms way as well as remaining true to their faith and morality, but another more significant influence was a constant companion to the Civil War soldier, his peers. Because many regiments during the early years of the war were raised from local communities and made up of boyhood friends and acquaintances, the lads endured ever-present peer pressure. To the dismay of many loved ones back home, however, this pressure often led in the wrong moral direction.

Regiments tended to be made up predominantly of young men from age seventeen to twenty-five. Such young men likely encouraged each other into misbehavior just as young men do in other times with taunts of being scared or being a coward if the young man in question did not comply. Such egging on probably was not really necessary for a group of young men away from home for the first time and largely left to their own devices. Furthermore, the need to "prove" their masculinity to themselves and their comrades created a tremendous amount of internal pressure to follow through with a visit to a prostitute. With money periodically in their pockets, a group of friends, and newfound freedom, large numbers of men from both armies frequented brothels, gambling dens, bars, and any other institutions that likely would have shocked the folks back home.

The complexities of the relationships between soldiers and prostitutes provide numerous areas for exploration. The reasons that soldiers visited prostitutes and the issues that they wrestled with in doing so reflected a range of views and concerns. Many Civil War soldiers did not receive regular visits by the paymaster. In light of this, they found a multitude of ways to pay for the services of prostitutes—some of which would earn a court-martial. In addition to the risk of military justice, soldiers also faced the possibility of contracting a venereal disease. Although no effective cures existed in during the war years, soldiers and surgeons attempted to treat the diseases with various concoctions. The prostitutes in varied locales—rural and urban areas—practiced their trade differently, with soldiers adapting negotiation practices and their efforts to seek out sex workers. Finally, the soldiers in the land armies of the Civil War had somewhat dissimilar experiences than the sailors in the navies in relation to prostitution. Although soldiers did not have constant access to women, especially during a campaign, sailors endured further limits on their efforts to engage sex workers. Among sailors, however, blockaders along the coast experienced access to vice much differently than their river-patrolling counterparts.

Accounts of soldiers involved with prostitutes during the war are limited because the men seldom mentioned such activities. Although military records, court-martial records, individual letters, and diaries reveal narrow glimpses of the debauchery occurring in camps and towns during the war, newspaper editors provided more information on such activities. Though editors quickly pointed out the excesses of enemy soldiers, they understandably proved reluctant to reveal the same offenses among their own troops. Knowing that newspapers often found their way across the lines, editors tried to avoid giving fodder to the public of the opposing side for its propaganda machines. Curiously, editors freely documented issues with prostitutes in their respective cities with scant clues as to their regular clientele. At times, the extent of the propaganda printed in newspapers from both regions became almost laughable. A fantastic example of this appeared in the *Daily Richmond Whig* on May 9, 1862. The editor related the story of a sixteen-year-old Confederate soldier wounded at Corinth, Mississippi. Surgeons later amputated the boy's leg. When he awoke he reportedly reacted with the following statement: "First rate! That old leg has bothered me since I was born. I've had it broken twice and laid in bed six months with a sprained knee. It has been a d----d [omission in original] unlucky leg anyhow, but now I'll have a wooden one, and the Yankees may shoot at that all day."[5] Though not as profound, reporting on prostitution showed similarly peculiarities. With hundreds and sometimes thousands of reported prostitutes in towns and cities, the women catered largely to the soldiers. By usually omitting such information, the local papers did not impugn the morality of their respective soldiers.

Just as newspaper editors on each side lauded the bravery of their own soldiers, they mocked the morals of their enemies. Under the title "Yankee Morals," the *Daily Richmond Whig* quoted a letter from another Confederate soldier at Corinth. The soldier claimed that the Confederates captured a number of offensive private letters from Union soldiers. "There were many letters found written by Yankee soldiers to their own families, so obscene that our roughest soldiers refused to read them aloud to their comrades; and just of such characters, too, were their letters from home."[6] According to the paper, not only were Union soldiers immoral, but they were also far worse than the most immoral soldiers that the Confederacy had to offer. In another dramatic insult for the time, the writer at the same paper charged: "The fact is, the Yankees are very little better than Chinese. They lay the same stress on the jingle of their dollars that the Celestials do on the noise of their gongs."[7]

Another newspaper, the *Memphis Daily Appeal*, claimed that Union soldiers encamped in Washington acted disorderly on several occasions.[8] A few months later in August 1861, the *Daily National Intelligencer* of Washington, D.C., seemed to admit to the charges but argued that the soldiers behaved themselves after being "brought under wholesome discipline." In the same issue, the editors of the *Intelligencer* quickly reported on Confederate behavior problems, citing an example of the 4th Alabama's wanton destruction of private property in a recent event.[9]

Although newspaper editors argued that the troops of the opposing nation behaved in a negative manner, in truth, both armies included young men who engaged in questionable behaviors. The soldiers of each army were not likely any more moral or immoral than their counterparts. A great many soldiers during the war sought out gambling, alcohol, and prostitutes, among a wide variety of other vices. Although soldiers of both armies delighted in the company of prostitutes, Union soldiers probably proved more successful in their efforts of procuring sex than their Confederate counterparts. Historian Bell Wiley concluded: "The men in blue were better paid, drew more generous bounties and had easier access to large cities than those who wore the gray."[10] Given the same resources and opportunities, it seems probable that a great many Confederates would have procured the services of ladies of the evening.

In addition to their newfound freedom, another factor contributing to the hedonistic behavior became the growing fatalism exhibited by soldiers during the war. "A battlefield offers the extreme challenge to the belief that one can control his fate," explained historian James McPherson. "Like rain, shells and bullets fall on the just and unjust alike. Soldiers quickly become fatalists."[11] The knowledge that death could be imminent had profound effects on soldiers during the period. Some soldiers adopted a "live for now" mentality and clearly engaged in the life that accompanied that state of mind. A significant minority, however, chose to live as chaste a life as possible in hopes that they would be spared eternal damnation if they were killed in combat. Following the battle of Cold Harbor, a member of the 4th Delaware Infantry wrote: "In that dreadful place . . . I resolved to forsake my evil ways and to serve god. I have done so and I pray the all-mighty to forgive me and make me pure from sin." Writing to his father, a Union private from Ohio scratched out: "I am trying to live a better man than I was at home. I see the necessity of living christian here where thy ar dropping all around you [sic]."[12]

Although the prospect of dying from a wound caused many to lead a somewhat hedonistic lifestyle, and led others to swear off any behavior that they regarded as sinful, most Civil War soldiers probably lived somewhere in between. Though they attempted to live a moral life, soldiers constantly faced temptation from vice as well as peer pressure from some comrades. In keeping with the duplicity of most human beings, probably the majority of soldiers during the Civil War occasionally indulged their whims to some degree and later felt remorse. Many soldiers seemed to be fence-sitters on the subject of morality. This notion is reflected in the numerous accounts of soldiers discarding the tools of vice before going into battle. On their way into a fight, soldiers dropped playing cards, dice, and nude pictures, among other items. By this simple act they avoided having the trappings of vice on them in the event of their death. If the soldier was lucky enough to survive the battle unscathed, he might retrieve his possessions when departing from the field, unless someone else picked them up first.[13]

Soldiers typically omitted such behavior in the letters sent to friends and relatives back home. If letters arrived with questionable content, recipients or descendents often destroyed the evidence of the soldier's "immorality." Fortunately, some letters still exist that document the lecherous inclinations of soldiers in blatant words as well as more obscure ramblings. One of the most widely known accounts containing a possible double meaning is the memoir of Confederate Sam Watkins. In his retelling, Watkins wrote that he and several others had a meal with a family with "two handsome daughters." Watkins described the meal in detail but focused on the butter. He claimed that at the end of the meal he was offered extra butter. After initially refusing, one of the daughters stated, "Mother, the gentleman don't wish butter." To which the mother replied, "Well, I want him to know that our butter is clean, anyhow." Feeling the overt encouragement of the mother, Watkins takes some butter.

> I dive in. I go in a little too heavy. The old lady hints in a delicate way that they sold butter. I dive in heavier. . . .The old lady says, 'We sell butter to the soldiers at a mighty good price.' I dive in afresh. She says, 'I get a dollar a pound for that butter,' and I remark with a good deal of nonchalance, 'Well, madam, it is worth it,' and dive in again. I did not marry [either] one of the girls.[14]

Several historians have claimed that Watkins' reference to selling butter is a euphemism for selling sex. His seemingly strange comment about not marrying either one of the girls possibly suggests this. An expectation of marriage following a complementary meal seemed to be an exceptionally high price to pay. Whether Watkins was discussing butter literally or attempting to camouflage a sexual encounter, his prose suggests an incredibly surreal event.

Whereas Watkins left his words up for debate in their actual meaning, other authors left little question in their subject matter. One federal infantryman in City Point, Virginia, commented in 1864: "We cannot get any thing [sic] here but f—king and that is plenty." Garrison work, although usually quite boring, evidently had its benefits for the federals at City Point. This did not represent a unique situation though because as occupying armies moved through the South and established garrisons, numerous prostitutes quickly descended on the area and set up shop. Other men attempted to be somewhat more subtle; a soldier from Massachusetts campaigning in Virginia in 1863 stated: "I had a gay old time I tell you. Lager Beer and a horse and Buggy [and] in the evening Horizontal Refreshments or in Plainer words Riding a Dutch gal—had a good time generally I tell you."[15] Although such visits to prostitutes occurred with some regularity, certain times instilled a carnival like atmosphere of vice. Because their respective paymasters often visited the troops at irregular intervals, such occasions became scenes of intense debauchery. During the Atlanta Campaign, John Bennitt, M.D., wrote home to his wife that he was recently paid for the first time in ten months and estimated that he would probably not "received any more pay within six months, and perhaps not till the end of my time of service."[16] Though Bennitt did not take part in the ribald celebrations, large groups of soldiers did just that. With ready cash in their pockets, many soldiers dashed to the brothels, red light districts, and taverns. August Scherneckau, a soldier serving with the provost guard, claimed: "as always after payday and also today there were drunks already." He went on to say, "since payday, most of them are staggering from one drunken stupor to another. I only hope that it does not last very long."[17] In addition to visits by the paymaster, other events, such as national holidays or major military victories, also served as an excuse for mass celebrations.[18]

One frank admission also revealed the extent that race played in the sex trade. Federal soldier, George Bates wrote from Beaufort, South Carolina, documenting his disappointment in the lack of white prostitutes. He claimed that there is "nothing but these damn negro wenches. I can't get it hard to go to them."[19] Union forces captured the Sea Islands of South Carolina, of which Beaufort is a part, early in the war. As the federals advanced on the islands, the white citizenry fled abandoning their slaves and free blacks to their fates. Although the African Americans on the islands had access to the food stores at the plantations that they lived on, as the whites fled, they likely took with them as many supplies as they could carry, which left the abandoned African Americans in relatively poor circumstances. Later, Bates felt relieved as white prostitutes began to arrive in the area. Many of the new arrivals were rumored to have venereal diseases, however, so Bates and his comrades still faced a quandary.[20]

A similar situation occurred in Nashville, Tennessee. After Provost Marshal George Spalding had many of the white prostitutes removed from the city, African American prostitutes established themselves in the newly vacated brothels. Spalding had only removed the immediate supply of sex workers, the demand by the soldiers was still present, which was a situation that Spalding could not control. Though many Union soldiers found white prostitutes more desirable, their absence forced soldiers to compromise and seek out the services of African American women.

George Scudder wrote to his friend Charles Tubbs concerning his troubles over having very little contact with white women. Scudder stated: "I have not see [sic] a White girl, Young lady, or Woman since Nov. except at a distance. When I go home I will fear them more than Gulliver did his wife after returning from his last voyage." He declared that after his return home he "would try and Stomach a kiss from a Mild nice looking Young Lassie providing she had no paint on her cheek or lips."[21]

Though a handful of these blatant accounts by soldiers describing the sex trade exist, the small number gives the impression of overall morality/civility among Civil War soldiers. The lack of evidence is misleading. Although soldiers censored themselves, or their relatives later censored their words, the exponential growth in the numbers of prostitutes in areas with soldiers attests to the notion that a large number of soldiers patronized the women. As occupying armies moved through the South, they established garrisons. Shortly thereafter, prostitutes flocked to the cities and found working arrangements. "Every occupied city became a haven of vice" according to Wiley, simply because of the number of young men willing to pay for sex matched with thousands of starving female Southerners.[22] For example, the population of prostitutes in Nashville, Tennessee, before federal occupation was around two hundred. Nearly thirty thousand Union soldiers arrived following the city's occupation on February 25, 1862. Soon afterward, approximately six to seven hundred prostitutes arrived in Nashville, hoping to cater to the newly arrived Yankees.[23] The venture proved to be an overwhelming success, so much so, that the garrison commanders in Nashville, and later at Memphis, instituted a program to keep in check the spread of venereal diseases.

Despite any limits that officers placed on soldiers, the enlisted men still found ways to obtain the services of prostitutes. Though some officers attempted to enforce unit regulations baring the men from brothels, saloons, or any places that prostitutes frequented, the larger issue for soldiers became paying for the services of the women. The federal paymasters visited the troops without much regularity. The troops stationed near cities or in established garrisons could expect more regular visits, but those soldiers in a campaigning army could not count on visits by the paymaster with any degree of certainty. When the paymaster did visit, the soldiers almost universally engaged in a wild celebration.[24]

The most serious problem associated with the sex trade was that of venereal diseases. Because physicians and scientists had not yet discovered the properties of antibiotics, people who contracted a venereal disease endured symptoms of that disease for the rest of their lives. Although

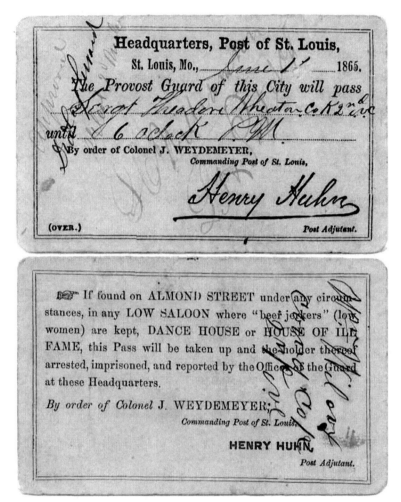

A pass for a soldier barring them from any venues that featured women engaging in prostitution. The logic behind this restriction was likely moralistic or an attempt to prevent the transmission of venereal disease. Courtesy of Elizabeth Topping.

on the surface, a venereal disease might not have seemed like much of a problem for anyone other than the unfortunate individual soldier, that idea was quite misleading. The major symptoms of syphilis typically do not manifest themselves for varying periods of time—anywhere from several months to several years—but other diseases such as gonorrhea and orchitis display symptoms rather quickly—within two to five days for gonorrhea.[25] Surgeons of the mid-nineteenth century often believed that, in the case of syphilis, once the primary chancre healed the patient was completely cured. Although they knew that some syphilitics relapsed later, most surgeons remained unaware that the initial chancre was only a symptom of the initial infection and not indicative of anything beyond that, including fighting off the disease.[26] In the Union Army: "during most months between two and four men in every thousand sought treatment for syphilis; a slightly higher number contracted gonorrhea. . . . In all, 73,382 cases of syphilis and 109,397 cases of gonorrhea and orchitis were treated in an army" with a total enlistment of 2.5 million soldiers during the war years.[27] These numbers reflect only the soldiers who actually sought out treatment for infections. A variety of circumstances, from embarrassment to fear, likely kept many infected soldiers from seeking treatment from regimental surgeons. Though, for the most part, gonorrhea and orchitis are rarely life-threatening, both infections are extremely painful. Requiring infected soldiers to march long distances, ride horseback, and fight in both hot and cold conditions proved almost futile. The pain associated with gonorrhea or orchitis greatly inhibited infected soldiers' capacity to serve.

As more and more soldiers succumbed to these infections, the gravity of the situation became obvious. Widespread infection had the potential to compromise the fighting ability of the militaries of both sides. Individuals, and occasionally military commanders, sought to cure venereal infections or even prevent them.[28] As the war dragged on, and more cases of venereal disease occurred, individual manufacturers of "cures" grew rapidly. Soldiers had the opportunity, depending on their locale, for purchasing a concoction dubbed "Blue Mass," which was produced by R. B. Saunders of Chapel Hill, North Carolina, with a third of its content being mercury.[29] Other peddlers, seeking to exploit every possible niche, also catered to advocates of natural cures. Advertisements for Brentlinger's Fluid Extract of Sarsaparilla and Dandelion claimed that the product was a "purely vegetable preparation" that cured rheumatism, headache, and most importantly "Syphilitic or Mercurial Diseases."[30] In addition to the naturalists, the *Memphis Daily Appeal* advertised

Medicines.

Glad News for the Unfortunate!

THE LONG SOUGHT FOR

DISCOVERED AT LAST.

CHEROKEE REMEDY

AND

CHEROKEE INJECTION,

Compounded from Roots, Barks and Leaves.

CHEROKEE REMEDY, the great Indian Diuretic cures all diseases of the urinary organs, such as Incontinence of the Urine, Inflammation of the Bladder, Inflammation of the Kidneys, Stone in the Bladder, Stricture, Gravel, Gonorrhea, Gleet, and is especially recommended in those cases of Fluor Albus, (or Whites in females,) where all the old nauseous medicines have failed.

☞ It is prepared in a highly concentrated form, the dose only being from one to teaspoonfuls three times per day.

☞ It is diuretic and alterative in its action ; purifying and cleansing the blood, causing it to flow in all of its original purity and vigor; thus removing from the system all pernicious causes which have induced disease.

CHEROKEE INJECTION is intended as an ally or assistant to the Cherokee Remedy, and should be used in conjunction with that medicine in all cases of Gleet, Gonorrhea, Fluor Albus or Whites. Its effects are healing, soothing and demulcent; removing all scalding, heat and pain, instead of the burning and almost unendurable pain that is experienced with nearly all the cheap quack Injections.

☞ By the use of the CHEROKEE REMEDY and CHEROKEE INJECTION—the two medicines at the same time—all improper discharges are removed, and the weakened organs are speedily restored to full vigor and strength.

☞ Price, Cherokee Remedy, $2 per bottle, or three bottles for $5.

☞ Price, Cherokee Injection, $2 per bottle, or three bottles for $5.

☞ Sent by Express to any address on receipt of price.

☞ For full particulars get our pamphlet from any drug store in the country, or write us and we will mail free to any address, a full treatise.

All such orders must be sent to C. A. COOK, Chicago, our General Agent for the West. P. O. Box 6324.

Sold in Chicago, by FULLER, FINCH & FULLER, Wholesale Druggists, and by all Druggists everywhere.

C. A. COOK, CHICAGO. General Agent for the States of Illinois, Iowa, Wisconsin, Michigan and Indiana.

Dr. W. R. MERWIN & CO.,

SOLE PROPRIETORS,

No. 59 Liberty street, New York.

THE GREAT

INDIAN MEDICINE,

COMPOUNDED FROM

ROOTS, BARKS  AND LEAVES.

Cherokee Cure!

An unfailing cure for Seminal Weakness, Nocturnal Emissions, and all diseases caused by Self-Pollution, such as Loss of Memory, Universal Lassitude, Pains in the Back, Dimness of Vision, Premature Old Age, Weak Nerves, Difficulty of Breathing, Trembling, Wakefulness, Eruptions on the Face, Pale Countenance, Insanity, Consumption, and all the direful complaints caused by departing from the path of nature.

☞ This medicine is a simple vegetable extract, and one on which all can rely, as it has been used in our practice for many years, and with thousands treated, it has not failed in a single instance. Its curative powers have been sufficient to gain victory over the most stubborn case.

☞ To those who have trifled with their constitution, until they think themselves beyond the reach of medical aid, we would say, DESPAIR NOT! the CHEROKEE CURE will restore you to health and vigor, and after all quack doctors have failed!

☞ Price, $2 per bottle, or three bottles for $5, and forwarded by Express to all parts of the world.

☞ For full particulars, get a Circular from any Drug Store in the country, or write to the Agent, who will mail free to any one desiring the same, a full treatise, in pamphlet form.

All such orders must be sent to C. A. COOK, Chicago, our General Agent for the West. P. O. Box 6324.

Sold in Chicago, by FULLER, FINCH & FULLER. Wholesale Druggists, and by all Druggists everywhere.

C. A. COOK, CHICAGO, General Agent for the States of Illinois, Iowa, Wisconsin, Michigan and Indiana.

Dr. W. R. MERWIN & CO.,

SOLE PROPRIETORS.

No. 59 Liberty street, New York.

JOHN DEMOND and PENICK & LOVING, Agents, St. Joseph, Mo.

Doctor Merwin and a litany of other supposed physicians placed advertisements in newspapers selling remedies for various venereal diseases. Like most of the other medicinal treatments of the period, these pills likely did not work to cure the named diseases. Courtesy of The State Historical Society of Missouri.

the "Cherokee Remedy!" which claimed to use no "Mineral Poison or Nauseous Drugs" during preparation and was "nature's own remedy for Gonorrhea (Clap)." Understanding the embarrassment of contracting a venereal disease, the kind makers of the Cherokee Remedy, Potter & Merwin, stated of their product: "It can lay on the toilet table, or in the counting room, without it ever being suspected as a remedy for private diseases."[31]

Another method that soldiers used to avoid venereal infections was condoms. Soldiers could procure condoms typically through mail-order advertisements in newspapers and from local shops, although with some degree of difficulty as far as their location. Advertisements for the items appeared with quite colorful language, as well as revealing some of the misunderstandings of disease for the period. D. E. Young of Philadelphia published an ad stating that "single men may use [condoms] to prevent themselves from becoming diseased when having intercourse with women of public character."[32] Other ads that promoted the belief that men could not control themselves sexually catered to both soldiers and traveling civilians. Doctor Jefferson B. Fancher described condoms for the "many married men, whose business calls them from home, are liable to accidents, and for the protection of their innocent *better halves* [italics in original], if not themselves, should neglect no safeguard; for surely no man could be so base as to entail upon his bosom companion a loathsome disease."[33] Although merchants made condoms available to males during the war, many soldiers unfortunately either did not have access to them or failed to see the possible consequences of their actions.

Command reacted in more complex ways. Because no official policy existed for either the Confederate or Union military on the matter, the ranking officer in a locale frequently dictated whether his men could patronize prostitutes. Generals such as Daniel Sickles, Joseph Hooker, Judson Kilpatrick, and perhaps Ulysses S. Grant felt that seeking out the company of prostitutes was a private matter in which the military should not be involved. With the exception of Grant, the actions of those generals may have actually encouraged the trade.[34] On the opposite end of the spectrum, Generals George McClellan, Joseph Johnston, Leonidas Polk, and Thomas "Stonewall" Jackson opposed the sex trade. A variety

TO THE PUBLIC.

GENTLEMEN:

I keep a Fancy and Variety Store at No. 703 Chesnut Street, Philadelphia, Pa., and have kept store in that Street ever since the year 1830, and have sold the article I am about to describe in the city of Philadelphia during the whole of that time ; as to the nature of the article, they are called CUNDUMS, or *Preventatives;* they are used for a private purpose by males, when having intercourse with the opposite sex.   The object in using them is as follows: Single young men use them to prevent themselves from becoming diseased when having intercourse with women of a public character; but where I sell one for the above purpose, I sell a hundred for domestic use, for the husband to use with his wife.   The object for there use in a domestic way is various.   The first and most important object is, to save the lives of thousands of wives, the husbands of whom would not lose them for the whole world, besides, as many females have some malformation by nature, which prevents them from having a child, without losing the life of one or both.   Now as nature has constructed us human beings pretty much all alike, as regards to the opposite sexes to have intercourse each with the other, it would be almost impossible to avoid the above lamentable results, without the use of something as a preventative, and Physicians recommend the above named articles very highly in such cases as just mentioned. They are also used in cases where child birth is not quite so severe as above stated, but where the wife has children so fast and so many of them, that it entirely breaks up and impairs her constitution, and disables her from doing duty better to a smaller number.   Indeed, many a man is sorely grieved to see the idol of his heart and companion for life wasting away before him, from the fact of her having children so fast, in such a case as last stated; this can be regulated to have children no faster than the wife's constitution will bear.   These Preventatives are also a safe guard for people in poor circumstances, and who find no pleasure in raising subjects for alms houses, poor houses, or work houses, or to be a tax upon the people.

Now, taking all the reasons together given above for the use of the within mentioned preventative, it certainly goes to show that the old saying is a true and a good one the world over." That one ounce of prevention is worth a pound of cure." The proper manner of using the preventative is, that when the sexual member of the male is in a proper condition for the purpose, he then takes one of these preventatives and draws it on said member, like you would the finger of a glove ; let it be dry till you get it on; after it is on, you put your hand into a pitcher or basin that has water in it, and run the penis once or twice through your closed up hand, for the purpose of making it stick or adhering to the penis.   The string is not for the purpose of tying, but to keep the article from splitting in putting it on, also, do not draw it on too close up at the point of the penis, but let the end of the preventive be about a half an inch from coming up to the end of the penis Indeed, all wives when they become acquainted with this article, they become strong advocates for the husband to use the preventative with them, and they certainly show their good sense in doing so, for the wife saves her own health, and can have just as many children as they can comfortably raise, and need not have any more than they think fit.

This circular you can show or give to any of your acquantances or friends that you think proper   All transactions or purchases of this article in your place will take place between the customer and your Postmaster, as I have as pointed him my agent in your place for this article if he thinks proper, but should he not feel inclined to transact this affair, any person seeing this, and wishing some of the article for use, can send to me direct for them, as below.

PRICE:—$3.00 per single paper or dozen.   For two dozen, $5,00.   For five dozen, $10,00.   Also on hand Yarners or Ticklers, at $3.00 per dozen.
Yours, respectfully,

Mr DE YOUNG.
No· 703 CHESTNUT STREET.
One door above 7th, North Side,
PHILADELPHIA, PA.

Condom advertisement. Such ads appeared in many newspapers, unfortunately, the advertised condoms were fairly expensive lower-ranking enlisted soldiers.
Advertisement courtesy of Elizabeth Topping.

of reasons created opposition, though. Rather than a religious or moral stand, McClellan and Johnston seemed to counter the trade from a viewpoint of maintaining fighting strength.[35]

Although regimental surgeons concerned themselves with venereal disease, other more immediate matters often vied for their attentions. Scurvy seemed to be foremost in the thoughts of regimental surgeons J. Franklin Dyer, M.D., and Bennitt, as well as other officers on both sides.[36] As early as March 1862, Dyer complained of scurvy among the men. That November he claimed that "if the men had not, in spite of orders, stolen all the vegetables they could

Period Condom. Although condoms were available through mail order, they required substantial planning ahead to procure such goods. Condom image courtesy of Civil War Medical Museum.

get (from the ground) not one would have escaped scurvy. Some of McClellan's favorites, Fitz John Porter's corps, and others fared very well, while others starved."[37] A few months previously, Dyer wrote to headquarters attesting to issues of scurvy in his brigade. In his journal he quoted the reply from the headquarters of the army as saying: "The troops should not have scurvy. Their rations are plentiful and good. Therefor [sic] scurvy does not exist."[38] Just as headquarters ignored Dyer's protestations about growing problems with scurvy, they also likely would have ignored problems with venereal disease had it been brought to their attention. In a medical hierarchy, however, scurvy threatened to debilitate many more soldiers than syphilis, gonorrhea, and orchitis combined. Because the army did not concern itself with the more pressing issue of scurvy at the time of Dyer's plea, there was little chance that the headquarters of the army would grant venereal disease any scrutiny. Unable to procure fresh fruits and vegetables from the Commissary Department, Bennitt resorted to calling on the Sanitary Commission and Christian Commission to prevent scurvy. Both groups provided Bennitt's men with produce several times during the Atlanta Campaign.[39]

Though soldiers stationed in garrisons near cities could pay prostitutes with money for the most part, those armies in the field campaigning usually did not have access to coin or paper money. As most rural prostitutes were "plying their trade" as a means of procuring food or shelter and most soldiers did not have ready cash, bargaining seemed to be a central part of the trade. Judging from surviving accounts—letters and court-martial records—penniless soldiers often stole provisions from the quartermaster stores to pay for the services of prostitutes. When they had access to the military stores, soldiers routinely stole items. In a letter to his brother, a Union soldier revealed one such trade. "We stole about a half a barrel of sugar and a box of cornmeal and traded them off for skin at the whore house." Other soldiers stole any number of valuable items such as coffee, bacon, and even whiskey to trade them for the services of prostitutes. [40]

Paying prostitutes through food and other supplies proved beneficial to the women as well. Reverend Francis Springer served as a Union chaplain in Arkansas with the provost guard. Springer extensively noted the conditions facing the local population. On January 1, 1863, he stated that "countless hundreds of men, women, and children roam in rags and beggary; the worst propensities of human nature—deception, uncleanness, thievery and violence."[41] Springer's words allowed for a more sympathetic viewpoint of why destitute women might trade sex for food. "The hay & fodder, as well as nearly all the corn on their respective farms, together with their best horses, were all taken by the scouts or foraging parties of either the Federal or Confederate armies."[42] Understanding the issue, some larger municipalities established relief organizations to provide shelter and food to impoverished women during the war years.[43]

Efforts by soldiers to seek out the company of prostitutes, either through smuggling them into camp or seeking their services in the local civilian population, and even stealing supplies to pay them, did not go unnoticed by army commanders who prosecuted a number of accused soldiers through court-martial. Fortunately for many soldiers, the priority of fighting the war left many military judges unable to impose overly harsh sentences. After authorities in Washington, D.C., discovered that Captain Jerome B. Taft of the 86th New York Volunteers secured an enlistment for his mistress by dressing her as a male, the provost marshal charged Taft with misuse of rank and theft, probably for supplying his mistress with supplies and provisions. Taft's sentence simply consisted of being dismissed from service.[44] A provost marshal sentenced a teamster named Joseph Meekins to forfeiture of pay for an undisclosed length of time for being in a brothel without authorization.[45] Most of these charges seem to involve other offences in addition to being in the company of a prostitute. Because additional charges usually complicated the picture, it is often difficult to judge how much of a particular sentence stemmed from the charges concerning prostitutes. One such convoluted case focused on Private H. C. Steel of the 3rd Illinois Cavalry. The provost marshal in Memphis charged Steel with bringing a suspected prostitute into camp dressed as a man, as well as being AWOL for a several days—allegedly in the company of the woman. Authorities sentenced Steel to sixty days at hard labor and forfeited his pay for that time period.[46] A number of factors had the strong potential to influence such disparity in the sentences for roughly the same infraction. Because there was no military-wide policy addressing the sex trade and military commanders largely dictated local policy regarding the trade, enforcement of prohibitive orders possibly came with some discretion. Though some commanders completely barred soldiers from consorting with prostitutes, given demands for manpower in both armies, overly harsh punishments that drained units of manpower for a seemingly minor issue probably remained rare. The provost marshal seemed to mete out such punishment to Meekins. The punishment for Taft and Steel reflected the additional charges that they faced, theft, misuse of rank, and being absent without leave.

Scherneckau, a soldier with the 1st Nebraska Infantry, voiced his frustration with chasing lecherous soldiers as a member of the provost guard in his journal. Scherneckau's unit acted in a more strict fashion than other authorities. According to the soldier, they once confronted several gamblers "and a quantity of cards, dice, etc., [were] confiscated."[47] Scherneckau noted that many illicit establishments possessed secret exits that enabled men to escape undetected. After arresting several men without passes in a St. Louis theater, the guard visited "all kinds of public houses without further results. Everyone who had no pass knew how to disappear one way or another as we approached."[48]

The US Sanitary Commission did not view kindly the inability of the provost guard and officers to look properly after their soldiers. "A loose impression prevailed that volunteers should not be controlled by the ordinary methods of military discipline."[49] The report went on to claim that newly commissioned officers were unable and incompetent to attend to the health of their men. The writer of the report expressed criticism about the transition period between enlistment and actual "transfer to the General Government." During this period, regimental surgeons and the larger medical department offered little supervision to their charges.[50] Charles Stille, the author of the report, charged that without supervision and guidance, many soldiers became "victims of diseases which have always proved the scourge of armies."[51]

Unfortunately, a clear comparison of Union and Confederate patrons of prostitutes is not possible. Fires consumed the majority of Confederate records at the close of the war in Richmond, including much of the Confederate military medical records. It is most likely that Union soldiers frequented prostitutes more often than their Confederate counterparts. This assertion is not based on the morality of Northern soldiers, but rather on their ability to obtain the company of prostitutes. The federal paymasters visited Union troops more regularly than their Confederate counterparts. The frequency of these visits still did not supply enough money for some men. Billy Murphy of the 141st Pennsylvania Infantry resorted to borrowing a dollar from Private Joel Molyneax to purchase alcohol.[52] The local origins of Northern units also seemingly made a difference in their rates of infection. Previous historians have argued that "the incidence of disease was especially heavy among new units composed largely of rural men passing through metropolitan centers in route to the front."[53] Though military medical records would lead one to believe that most infections occurred in those units from rural areas, presumably as a result naiveté, this is misleading. It is much more probable that, although rural soldiers experienced a higher rate of initial infection on entering military service, many soldiers from urban areas probably already had experience with venereal diseases. Such knowledge came either through direct contact from a personal infection or indirect contact through the experience of an associate. Urban soldiers used their prior contact with venereal diseases as a warning to avoid prostitutes or simply did not seek military medical attention because their private efforts to find a cure had failed. In both situations, more soldiers hailing from urban areas knew how to procure private treatments and avoid the terribly painful treatments that regimental surgeons administered. Ultimately, through their own efforts, soldiers from urban areas created the false impression that they visited prostitutes with much less regularity than their rural comrades.

White soldiers on the whole had fairly regular access to regimental surgeons. African American soldiers and sailors experienced a different level of medical care. The US Colored Troops (USCT) endured a mortality rate of two and a half times that of white troops. Only a "couple hundred white and a few black physicians" attended to the entire contingent of black soldiers—179,000 men.[54] Recruiters found it difficult to procure surgeons to serve with the USCT. Whites usually did not want to attend to the medical needs of African Americans, and the army proved reluctant to commission African Americans in the regular army. The potential for African American surgeons to operate on white soldiers during battle as well as the possible implications of lower-ranking whites saluting African American officers would not have held with the societal norms of the period. The medical department faced such difficulties in recruiting qualified medical staff, such as assistant surgeons; officials used former orderlies as assistant surgeons. Eventually, several officers "arranged an early graduation program with selected medical schools for students who agreed to enter the USCT."[55]

Many of the limited numbers of surgeons that treated African American soldiers believed some of the prevalent stereotypes of the period. The belief that African Americans were inherently lazy caused many surgeons to dismiss cases of illness or ailments.[56] Occasionally, the lack of medical care proved beneficial to African American troops. Medical thinking prescribed poisonous mercury or even opium for some diseases. Surgeons sent whites to hospitals, however, where they recovered in a sanitary environment. African American soldiers, when they gained admission to an army hospital, went to segregated and frequently filthy facilities.[57]

Conversely, African American sailors had a much different experience with surgeons and the navy's medical department. Nearly every US ship had a "full-time medical officer present." On the whole, the navy had a much better medical department than the army. In 1861, the navy had five hospitals and the army had only one.[58] African American soldiers obtained better medical care in the navy than their infantry comrades. Because only one surgeon existed on most ships, African American sailors received the same level of care as white soldiers.[59] Given the close quarters onboard ships, crews had little choice but to get intimately acquainted with their fellow sailors through conversations covering every aspect of their lives. In this light, many sailors, surgeons, and captains found it more difficult to treat African American sailors with racist hostility. Furthermore, the general conditions aboard navy ships benefited the health of sailors. These men had sheltered quarters rather than sleeping in the open, or at best usually in a tent, low incidents of scurvy, even lower than that of the army, and even had access to clean drinking water from the condensers that provided fresh water for the boilers.[60]

On the whole, rates of infection for African Americans remained much lower than that for whites during the war. The lower rate of infection likely resulted from a number of factors. White customers enjoyed access to both white as well as African American prostitutes, whereas social restrictions almost universally did not allow African

American soldiers to patronize white prostitutes. The USCT often served in less desirable and even less healthy areas prone to infections of malaria and yellow fever. With customers readily available in healthier regions, prostitutes probably did not wish to risk their lives in a business that ultimately centered on survival. Public scrutiny kept many African American soldiers from seeking out the company of prostitutes. The US public, both North and South, closely watched the fortunes and behaviors of African American soldiers. Understanding their precarious state, many African American soldiers and their commanders policed themselves and each other. Many African American soldiers still visited prostitutes with some contracting diseases and others entering service with a preexisting infection.

The ability to pay for services emerged as one of the most important aspects of the lives of African American soldiers that limited their access to prostitutes. From the time that they entered the army in 1863, the Army paid African American soldiers roughly half of what white soldiers received, until June 1864, when Congress acted to equalize the pay scale. The change did not occur immediately. In August 1864, a soldier from New York complained that the paymaster still only delivered seven dollars to each soldier for every month of service. The same soldier complained that the commissariat also frequently shorted the regiment on rations.[61] Thomas Sipple, a black soldier with the 20th New York, also wrote from Camp Parpit the same month to complain. Sipple addressed his letter to President Abraham Lincoln stating that his regiment had not been paid in seven months with a wife and three children needing his assistance at home.[62] The problem did not end with the conclusion of the war. A group of men from the 33rd USCT wrote to General Daniel Sickles in 1866 respectfully claiming that they spent most of their wages on supplemental food from sutlers because their rations proved insufficient.[63] Soldiers in the USCT rarely found sufficient wages or foodstuffs for themselves, let alone having surplus money or goods to purchase the services of prostitutes.

The actual numbers of infected whites far exceeded the number of infected African Americans, but because whites greatly outnumbered

African Americans in the army as a whole, percentages of infection are much more telling. Usually rates of infection with venereal diseases for black soldiers ran about 1,000 to 2,000 lower than white soldiers per 100,000 men. The only time that the African American rate of infection surpassed the white rate was in October 1862. That month the records indicate that surgeons recorded infections of 7,000 whites and 7,500 African Americans per 100,000 men.[64] The early spike in venereal disease among African American soldiers can be explained by their recent induction into the US Army. In what was probably their first time away from their home communities, the earliest black inductees journeyed to a training camp where prostitutes congregated, with many engaging in the same behavior as many new white soldiers. April 1864 saw a spike of infections for all soldiers with African Americans reaching 6,500 and whites at 10,000 per 100,000. In August those numbers dropped to the more average numbers of 5,000 African Americans and 7,000 whites. The peak in April may have been related to the concentrations of Grant's and William T. Sherman's armies near Washington and Chattanooga. Numbers continued to slightly decline until the end of the war with a tremendous climb following the surrender of Confederate forces in the summer of 1865, likely as a result of a more relaxed situation and more soldiers near Washington and Richmond.[65]

Although, a great number of soldiers visited prostitutes regularly or at least occasionally had access to them, ironically many sailors in the Union Navy could not consort with the women. A clear distinction within the Navy is warranted because those sailors serving in the blockading fleet had completely different experiences than those of the men serving on gunboats patrolling and fighting on the rivers of the Confederacy.

As the blockading fleet grew in the early years of the war, the US Navy desperately needed men to crew blockaders. The Navy appealed to sailors to join the blockading fleet by way of broadsides offering outstanding bonuses for captured blockade runners.[66] Although recruiters claimed that sailors would consistently capture them, blockade runners typically evaded the blockaders only granting the blockade sailors a fruitless rousing in the middle of the night.[67] Furthermore, as another

USS Sabine. *The* Sabine *was one of the many Union blockading ships that spent extended periods off the coast of the Southern states. The blockaders were often resupplied at sea because of the risk of sailors abandoning ship while in port.*

measure to keep sailors from deserting during one of the infrequent periods in port, the Navy did not pay the sailors a monthly wage or even distribute prize money for captured runners. The navy usually only distributed such earnings on a sporadic basis or even at the end of a sailor's enlistment.[68] Although the sailor only experienced some animosity directed at the Navy in general and specifically his officers, his family—if he had one—suffered the most. His family members did not even receive the pay earned by the sailor, however, and often were forced to support themselves rather than being able to depend on the supposed windfall from the Navy. Unfortunately, rather than being able to survive on the sailor's earnings, some wives and perhaps daughters of sailors engaged in prostitution, ultimately because of misguided policies put in place by the US Navy.[69]

Rather than getting frequent breaks onshore because of their close proximity to land, sailors on the blockade typically remained on their ships and in some cases, longer than merchant sailors voyaging from

California to China. Because captains denied their men access to port, blockading sailors did not typically contract venereal diseases because they had extremely limited access to prostitutes. The occasional appearance of women on the ships raised the men's morale significantly. Using them as a marketing tool, sutlers hired women to serve as clerks on boats selling items to men serving on the blockade. By using women, the sutlers could usually get higher prices for their goods as the sailors wished to keep the women on board as long as possible. Seaman Israel Vail captured the dumbfounded reactions of sailors on his ship: "The sight of a woman had been denied us for eight months, and we had only dim recollections of how they looked, and the sudden appearance of several of that sex upon our station nearly prostrated us with astonishment and delight. . . ."[70] With so little to break up the dreariness of the blockade, looking forward to a possible visit by a female clerk may have been the mental saving grace for many a sailor in the fleet.

Although many of the sailors serving on the Atlantic Blockade were likely career sailors, the sailors that served on the riverine gunboats of the Union Navy came from a completely different class of people. The gunboat squadrons had trouble obtaining recruits. As a result, the squadrons accepted men rejected by the blockade units as well as army "castoffs." By the end of the war, the riverine squadrons accepted escaped slaves and galvanized Confederate prisoners of war.[71] As a result of such recruiting practices, the men of the riverine squadrons earned a reputation as a much rowdier and more debaucherous set than their counterparts on the blockade or in the army. Once the sailors of the riverine gunboats went on board their boats, they had a clear advantage over their fellow sailors of the blockade: their proximity to land. Often, rather than several miles, gunboatmen were only several yards from the shore. Because of such proximity to land, these sailors had regular access to the prostitutes that operated in cities along the river.[72]

Many of the ports where gunboats docked for resupply had been in the business of catering to river traffic for a number of years. A fine example of one of these cities is Memphis, Tennessee. After the Union forces captured Memphis in June 1863, the city became a supply depot for the federals. This new incarnation for the city brought significant prosperity, especially for those working in businesses related to the transfer of goods along the river. One of the numerous industries catering to this traffic was prostitution. Along the waterfront in Memphis, sex workers lashed flatboats to the shore of the Wolf River—one of the Mississippi's offshoots—and operated floating brothels.[73] The sex trade proved such a booming business in Memphis and other river ports— especially New Orleans—that it supported a thriving patent medicine industry producing "cures" for venereal diseases. The *Memphis Daily Appeal* usually printed two or three advertisements for the cures on each of its pages devoted to advertisements.[74] Such ports attracted prostitutes as well as soldiers and sailors moving through the area. A captain from Ohio remarked: "Memphis . . . can boast of being one of the first places of female prostitution on the continent. Virtue is scarcely known within the limits of the city."[75] Although the captain commented on Memphis, as the war dragged on, more and more cities exhibited similar circumstances of more and more destitute women turning to prostitution to survive, along with more and more soldiers and sailors willing to pay for sex as the supply of available women grew and the price continued to drop.

Although many men did seek out the services of prostitutes— enough to support hundreds of women in towns and major cities such as Nashville—numbers of men avoided the sex trade. These men avoided the trade for several reasons: disease, remaining faithful to wives or girlfriends, and even a sense of morality. The soldiers who declined to consort with prostitutes because of a strong sense of morality often joined larger organizations, such as the US Christian Commission or the YMCA. Such groups spoke out against prostitution as well as alcohol, pornography, and vice among soldiers in general.[76]

Though historians cannot be sure exactly how many soldiers engaged in the sex trade during the Civil War, it is reasonable to conclude that the trade became widespread. Although the exact numbers involved in the trade cannot be known, there are clues to the extent. It is estimated that the population of prostitutes in Nashville reached six to seven hundred during the war. More than 109,000 Union soldiers contracted gonorrhea and more than 73,000 contracted syphilis.[77] These numbers stemmed from army medical reports, so they did not capture the full damage of venereal disease from the war. Many soldiers and sailors either did not seek treatment, choosing rather to endure their "embarrassing" disease privately, or sought a cure from a civilian doctor, possibly in an effort to resolve the problem discretely. Obviously a large number of soldiers sought out the company of ladies of the evening.

Civil War soldiers engaged in sordid activities for a number of reasons. Some soldiers found themselves overwhelmed with newfound freedom as they left the confines of their small town communities. The lack of oversight by the more refined members of the community, as well as encouragement by their peers, opened the way for young soldiers to discover and explore sources of vice before they returned home following the war. Other soldiers embraced a fatalistic outlook, believing that they would not return from the war. Such soldiers endeavored to live their lives to the fullest during their perceived short time left on earth. Soldiers visited both African American and white prostitutes during the war. Although some complained about the lack of white women, enough soldiers patronized African American sex workers to make it a viable survival option for those women during the war years. Prostitutes made soldiers' visits more accessible by accepting a variety of payments. Soldiers obtained such items through an assortment of avenues, many times stealing them from the quartermasters' stores. Unfortunately for the thieves, the provost guard and quartermasters readily court-martialed offenders.

Visits to prostitutes opened up soldiers to infections with venereal diseases. Gonorrhea and syphilis threatened to debilitate thousands of men and infect their wives and girlfriends following the war. Prostitutes unwittingly exacerbated the problem by accumulating near garrisons or even offering their services to passing armies and sporadically transferring venereal diseases as they conducted business. Once infected, soldiers sought out a variety of questionable treatments through regimental surgeons as well as on the private market. The army did not provide equal medical care for all soldiers, however. African American soldiers of the USCT did not receive even a fraction of the care provided to white soldiers. Nearly every disease faced by soldiers wreaked havoc to a much higher degree among African American soldiers with the exception of venereal diseases. Public scrutiny, lower availability of prostitutes, and undesirable service locales combined to limit the exposure of African American soldiers to venereal diseases. Infection rates proved to be lower among both African American and white sailors. Although those sailors serving on the blockade did not see prostitutes or land for months at a time, their occasional shore leaves provided rare access to women. Riverine forces, however, often found themselves mere feet from shore and frequently in river cities with reputations for lax social standards. Some army commanders attempted to stem the tide of infections by outright barring soldiers from brothels, whereas others attempted to control infections by regulating the trade. Still others chose to ignore the issue or focused on more pressing matters. For diverse reasons, significant numbers of soldiers during the Civil War had sexual relations with prostitutes, risking personal diseases and collectively threatening to prolong the war through the debilitation of thousands of men.

4
The General Officers

ust as Civil War soldiers differed on their views and patronizing of prostitutes, so too did the general officers commanding the men. Although a little older than their enlisted men, many general officers were still in their forties in 1861. Thus, men who attained the rank of general officer during the war did not come from an altogether different generation with morals and norms that varied from those of their men. The births of most general officers and soldiers occurred either during the waning years of the Second Great Awakening or soon thereafter. The parents of these men gradually distanced themselves—consciously or not—from the religious fervor that swept the country for years. Their children grew up as society reverted back to a more natural relationship with religion, which was neither overtly fanatical nor distant or agnostic, rather falling somewhere between the two extremes for most Americans. Because of the country's relaxed relationship with religion during its formative years, it is likely that many Civil War soldiers and officers had a relatively lenient view of prostitution and vice overall.

General officers tended to fall into three categories with regard to the sex trade—opposition, endorsement, or indifference. The majority of officers, believing that they had much more pressing war-related concerns, ignored the moral indiscretions of their soldiers. Some general officers opposed the sex trade on either religious or pragmatic grounds.

Gideon Welles, the Secretary of the US Navy, for example, likely opposed the sex trade among his sailors because of his Puritan heritage.[1] Those officers opposing prostitution for pragmatic reasons largely did so to prevent venereal diseases among their soldiers from debilitating their forces. Other officers, although not publicly endorsing the trade, either passively endorsed the trade by consorting with prostitutes themselves or allowed the trade to operate, understanding the impossibility of eradication. Officers who understood the impossibility of eliminating contact between prostitutes and soldiers allowed the trade to continue in a more controlled manner to prevent venereal disease. In a few cases, these officers implemented programs attempting to detect cases of venereal disease in prostitutes—usually gonorrhea or syphilis—and had surgeons treat these cases before allowing infected prostitutes to return to work. Furthermore, to the utter confusion and frustration of the soldiers, when a new general took command of their army, regulations concerning prostitution and other vices could change on the whim of the commanding officer. Complete reversals of regulations periodically occurred. The Army of the Potomac saw several dramatic shifts in philosophy with its numerous changes in command. Whatever their reasons for opposing, endorsing, or ignoring the issue of prostitution during the Civil War, the actions of general officers fit into the ongoing struggle over prostitution and other vices that was occurring in larger society.

The general officers presented a more extensive and comprehensive picture of the issue of prostitution during the war than did their men. Because general officers tended to be more prolific writers, their views appeared more frequently in newspapers and in military orders and reports. Stories concerning soldiers and prostitutes remained less common.

With the opening of the Civil War in the spring of 1861, the US officer corps divided according to the loyalties of its members. The Union officer corps became severely diminished, whereas the Confederate officer corps, though small, also faced the problem of completely establishing itself. These issues, coupled with the nearly insurmountable feat of hastily training hundreds of thousands of fresh recruits, left little time for general officers to concern themselves with recruits frequenting prostitutes. Rather than being concerned with the morals of their men, officers struggled to deal with the necessities of preparing their men for combat, as well as simply providing adequate food and shelter for waves of young men arriving from home. For the experienced officers of the antebellum army, this seemed an incredibly daunting prospect. Yet such officers had an advantage. Their prior experience in the army had given them the basic tools of organization, training, and experience to accomplish such goals, so that they "merely" had to increase the scale. Many of the new, inexperienced officers—most famously, the political appointees—felt completely overwhelmed by their new responsibilities. "Green" officers primarily inundated themselves with learning the norms and tactics of the regular army, as well as acclimatizing themselves to leading men into combat. With such incredible demands on them, many new officers found it impossible to look to the morality of their men in addition to attending to their responsibilities in preparing the men for battle.

Other officers, although concerned about vices such as prostitution, frequently attended to the most pressing of these issues. The Provost Marshal General for the Army of the Potomac, Marsena Rudolph Patrick, mainly concerned himself with reports of plundering by Union soldiers in the early months of 1862.[2] By May, he commented on the complete lack of discipline in the army: "Officers are a set of drones, generally & do not care a fig for discipline or duty."[3] The next month Patrick noted: the "men are indifferent & feel that they are acting without an object or a purpose; consequently they behave badly."[4] Whether on a campaign or back in camp outside Washington, D.C., Patrick found some issues to which he objected. On June 8, 1863, Patrick confiscated fake jewelry as well as "the vilest of Obscene Books, of which I have made a great haul lately." He later burned those and others taken from the mail.[5]

Even those general officers who tried to restrict their men from visiting prostitutes achieved varying degrees of success. As historian Lawrence Murphy noted: "Some military commanders were more conscientious and effective than others in keeping their men away from prostitutes or, as an alternative, assuring that prostitutes were free from venereal disease."[6] General Thomas J. "Stonewall" Jackson incredibly maintained

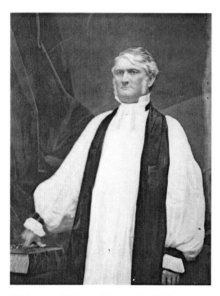

Bishop and General Leonidas Polk. Though Polk served primarily as a military leader during the war, he often took Sundays to lead his men in religious instruction.

strict morality in his camp. After a visit to Jackson's camp in May 1862, J. C. Clopton wrote: "During my stay among General Jackson's command I heard but little profanity and saw but little wickedness of any kind. . . . I was told the other day that Gen. Jackson himself was out distributing tracts among his men."[7] Clopton stated that those under Jackson's direct command kept a close eye on their vices, at least in the presence of the general. Confederate Lieutenant General Leonidas Polk, also known as the Fighting Bishop, preached the gospel as a bishop of the Episcopal Church before accepting a commission in the Confederate Army.[8] Polk held religion to be of the utmost importance. In private letters, he often called for more religion in camp as a benefit to the enlisted men.[9]

Union General Robert McAllister also held a strong aversion to vice. Reportedly, McAllister exhibited a strong reaction to alcohol even as a baby. Some parents of the period used the accepted practice of massaging ill babies with whiskey as a means of treatment. McAllister "always grew white and sick from such treatment." As he grew into adulthood, McAllister continued this natural repugnance to spirits and tried to impose his beliefs on his men.[10] As colonel of the 11th New Jersey Infantry, McAllister posted orders forbidding alcohol in camp. The order proved nearly impossible to enforce. "Some poor slave of appetite" for liquor usually occupied the guardhouse as a result of the order.[11] In an ironic twist, for at least part of his tenure as colonel, the 11th New Jersey regiment came under the command of the hard drinking General

Daniel Edgar Sickles. During the engagement in the Peach Orchard at Gettysburg, McAllister received a wound from one of General James Longstreet's men. After being evacuated to the rear, the colonel even refused whiskey from the attending surgeon. Finally the surgeon mixed some whiskey in McAllister's milk. "'He was heard afterward,' one soldier recollected, 'speaking in terms of praise of the milk given by the Gettysburg cows.'"[12]

Although Jackson and Polk discouraged their men from seeking out prostitutes and engaging in other vices for religious reasons, General George McClellan opposed the trade as only part of the larger discipline problem within the Army of the Potomac. In October 1861, McClellan ordered the Provost Guard in Washington, D.C., to cease issuing passes for relatives to visit soldiers in camp, publicly blaming the lack of discipline of the army.[13] Though on the surface, it seems that McClellan prohibited relatives from visiting soldiers as punishment for the behavior of soldiers, such an interpretation does not seem likely. Soldiers commonly claimed a prostitute as a wife or relative as a means of gaining her admission into camp. Enlisted men used the ruse to great effect in smuggling many women into their tents. Rather than overtly claiming that his soldiers brought prostitutes into camp, McClellan quietly removed one method of bringing in sex workers. Yet his efforts did not completely rid his command of prostitutes.

In addition to the lax discipline in the Army of the Potomac prior to his assignment as commander, McClellan may have had a personal issue with the ramifications of the sex trade. The woman McClellan married, Ellen Marcy, had a reputation in the 1850s as one of the most sought-after young ladies among the officers of her husband's generation. One lucky gentleman, A. P. Hill, began courting Marcy in 1855, and the couple became engaged to be married in the spring of 1856.[14] If Hill had simply been a former suitor of his wife, McClellan might not have given the issue much thought, but the courtship of Hill and Marcy may have had lasting affects. The problem stemmed from Hill's love of women. "Hill loved women generally. He had loved them when they were Latin beauties cannonading him with those angry flashing eyes from the balconies of Puebla. He loved them when they were Washington girls casting coquettish glances across the crowded public rooms at Willard's Hotel. He loved them under all circumstances."[15] Unfortunately, Hill's lust for women caused unforeseen consequences during a summer break from West Point. Although Superintendent Richard Delafield had warned his cadets not to spend any time in New York City on their trips home, Hill could not resist. His overpowering urges resulted in a case of gonorrhea after a visit to a local prostitute. Complications of the disease even forced Hill to push back his graduation date to 1847 rather than 1846.[16] It is unlikely, but Marcy may have contracted the disease from Hill during their engagement. If Marcy then had the disease, she most certainly passed it along to McClellan. No records have been discovered to attest to such a scenario however. Furthermore, Hill believed that Marcy's parents knew of the disease and forced her to break off the engagement. Hill stated: "my health and constitution had become so impaired, so weakened, that no mother could yield her daughter to me, unless to certain unhappiness."[17] Whether or not McClellan actually contracted the disease, he very likely knew of his classmate's infection, which granted him indirect knowledge of the problems associated with the disease. If he did contract gonorrhea and sought a cure from a private physician, no records of the treatment would likely exist. Hill sought the care of the physician at West Point, thereby, preserving his experience with the disease for posterity.

Confederate General Joseph E. Johnston also had plenty of knowledge concerning venereal diseases and prostitutes. His command became overwhelmed with sex workers and Johnston endeavored to remove them. In Dalton, Georgia, in early 1864 a Confederate officer in the Army of Tennessee wrote "Complaints are daily made to me of the number of lewd women in this town, and on the outskirts of the army. They are said to be impregnating this whole command, and the Commissariat has been frequently robbed with a view of supporting these disreputable characters."[18] Though the problem with stolen army supplies and the troublesome issue of prostitutes lingering about frustrated many officers, because soldiers were able to pay for services with provisions from the commissariat, it is more likely that these women were simply working to survive rather than being "lewd" or "disreputable characters." Confederate authorities attempted to remove the women from the vicinity of the army. To rectify the issue, Johnston ordered all women "who were not able to give proof of respectability and the means of an honest livelihood could be sent to points beyond the reach of soldiers."[19] In response to Johnston's order, Confederate officers had all suspected prostitutes removed from town and placed in the guardhouse with bread and water to sustain them.[20] As was the case with other attempts to remove the source of the disease problem, this effort probably did not work either. Other destitute women most certainly moved into the area and took up the trade because of the low supply and high demand for sex workers by the soldiers.

Union Brigadier General John Pope attempted to use the provost guard to police morality in Missouri just as Johnston had in Georgia. His use of the provost guard to address issues of morality proved unsuccessful. Pope then focused the provost on maintaining some semblance of order in the Union-occupied areas of the state. The men of the provost guard largely ignored prostitution and other vices to focus on safeguarding the lives of civilians.[21]

Pope's situation is very telling. Often officers who opposed the sex trade dealt with other problems that demanded their attention. Although issues of vice confronted commanders at Nashville, the problems remained of secondary importance until they grew to potentially disastrous levels. Shortly after the fall of Nashville to Union forces, newspaper editors published General Orders Number 6. The order stated: "Railroad companies, & the James River & Kanawha Canal Company are forbidden to transport into this city or out of it, spirituous liquors, or other intoxicating beverages."[22] One of the initial problems of many garrisons proved to be overindulgence on arrival in larger cities. As symptoms of venereal diseases usually lie dormant for at least a short time, the problem sometimes grew out of hand before the commander became aware of it. Historian James Jones argued that the "problem presented by prostitution and venereal disease was not planned for by the army, and it became a problem of major significance in Nashville and Memphis."[23] Nearly a year after General Orders Number 6, regimental commanders and medical officers forced General R. S. Granger to address the issue of prostitution and venereal disease. Although Granger likely did not promote or feel indifferent toward the trade, a plethora of other topics demanded his focus. Jones remarked: "Action was essential [however], 'to save the army from a fate worse . . . than to perish on the battlefield.' Prostitution itself, though physically harmless, led to venereal disease, and equally proved 'annoying and destructive to the morals of the army.'"[24] Eventually the situation demanded that Granger and other commanders in Nashville institute a system of licensing prostitutes as a means of controlling the spread of venereal diseases.[25]

Although Granger gave orders as a means of controlling venereal disease, the commander at Memphis enacted a similar program with additions seeking to control the behavior of the prostitutes themselves. Already known as a haven of vice prior to the war, Memphis carried an air of permissiveness prior to the Union occupation in 1862. Provost Marshal John H. Gould attempted to curtail the lax treatment of prostitution and other vices. As in Nashville, the provost guard tried to stem the tide of alcohol quickly after occupation on July 9, 1862. Eight days later, Gould issued an order stating: "Lewd women are prohibited from conversing with soldiers while on duty; nor will they be allowed to walk the streets after sunset. Anyone of the class indicated who shall violate this order will be conveyed across the river and will not be allowed to return within the limits of the city."[26]

Those orders did not remedy the concern because the provost marshal issued similar orders the following May. Special Order Number 13 stated that prostitutes could be sent North, members of the Union army caught in brothels could be arrested, and steamboat men bringing prostitutes into Memphis could face fines.[27] Even after the acceptance of the Nashville program of legalized prostitution in Memphis, the sex workers of Memphis lived with extensive restrictions on their behavior and movement around the city.[28]

The Army of the Potomac seemingly embraced vice under the command of General Joseph Hooker. Very low spirits plagued the army before Hooker's promotion to commander. "Most of the army had not been paid in six months or more." His men had no money to spend on themselves, and more importantly to send back home to their families. Hooker was "daily receiving letters from the latter representing their destitution and distress." Frustrated, Hooker responded by enforcing regular paymaster visits.[29] Although Washington newspapers did not report the situation, many of the newly wealthy soldiers with six months pay in their pockets may have engaged in widespread debauchery, hopefully retaining some money to send home to relatives.

Understanding that the men in the Army of the Potomac and many men in general, occasionally solicited the services of prostitutes, Hooker relocated many of the prostitutes in Washington, D.C., into a central "red light district." This move is one that a few historians have regarded as a "realistic policy toward recreation for the troops."[30] General Hooker took the same approach to his own entertainment as well. New Englander, Charles Frances Adams referred to Hooker's headquarters as "a place where no gentleman cared to go, and no lady could. It was a combination barroom and brothel." As his cavalry unit provided escort duty at the headquarters for a time, Adams had a thorough familiarity with its atmosphere.[31] General Sickles served as one of the men who helped General Hooker acquire that reputation. Sickles' reputation seemed to trump Hooker's. George Templeton Strong, one of the founders of the US Sanitary Commission, wrote of Sickles that "one might as well try to spoil a rotten egg as to damage Dan's character."[32]

Many people knew Sickles as a notorious character who regularly kept the company of prostitutes as far back as his years with Tammany Hall in his early twenties. A year after marrying Teresa Bagioli in 1852—a match opposed by both families—Sickles departed for London as the US Secretary of Legation. He opted to leave Teresa in the United States and took a prostitute and madam named Fanny White as his companion. While in London, Sickles used White to get back at James Gordon Bennett of the *New York Herald* who had lampooned Sickles as unfit for the post. Sickles introduced Fanny White to Queen Victoria as "Miss Bennett of New York," a move that infuriated Bennett. The

*Major General Joseph Hooker.
General Hooker worked to provide
a specific red light district in
Washington, D.C., to provide better
supervision for his men seeking the
company of prostitutes.*

*Major General Daniel Sickles.
General Sickles often consorted with
prostitutes even during his marriage.
During the war, Sickles continued to
harbor prostitutes at his camp.*

publisher retaliated in the *Herald* with attacks on Sickles for the next four years.[33]

Sickles returned to the United States, and after a few years in the New York Assembly, he won a seat in the US House of Representatives in 1857. While in Washington, Sickles continued his womanizing ventures as Teresa attempted to maintain the appearance of a representative's wife. As Sickles was busy with his congressional duties as well as his continued attentions to other women, he introduced Teresa to Phillip Barton Key, who would serve as her escort to Washington social gatherings. Key and Teresa engaged in an affair during which Key rented a house up the street from the Sickles' residence on Lafayette Square for afternoon rendezvous. Though Sickles continued to patronize prostitutes, when he found out about his wife's affair, the representative flew into a rage. He confronted Teresa and forced her to write out a lengthy and graphic confession. The next

Teresa Baglioli Sickles. Mrs. Sickles begun an affair with Philip Barton Key during her husband's time in Washington as a US Senator.

Philip Barton Key. Key initially served as a companion to Mrs. Sickles during her husband's frequent absences. Eventually, this relationship blossomed into an intimate affair.

The murder of Philip Barton Key. Upon discovering his wife's affair, Sickles charged from the home and shot Key on the street in full view of the public. He later claimed that he was overcome with rage and was not able to control himself.

time that Sickles saw Key, Teresa's lover surreptitiously waved his handkerchief as a signal for her to come to the rented house up the street.[34] Sickles charged from the house with two pistols and mortally wounded Key. Authorities apprehended Sickles and put him on trial in one of the most sensational murder trials of US history.[35] In a landmark move, Sickles' defense team won an acquittal using the first temporary insanity defense in US legal history. Surprisingly, the press as well as Sickles' defense attorneys lauded Sickles as a hero after the trial, with reports that he had struck a blow for fidelity and morality. Ironically, the prosecuting attorneys made no mention of Sickles' own problems with infidelity.[36]

As expected, Sickles continued his womanizing behavior as an officer in the US Army during the Civil War. Like Charles Adams' accusations of debauchery at headquarters, the Confederate press capitalized on Sickles' reputation during the war. Remembering the former representative's ties to Tammany Hall and other saucy exploits, the *Richmond Daily Whig* claimed that a group of soldiers deserted Sickles' New York Excelsior Brigade. Although the editor was not blatant in his accusation, he hinted that the general's past reputation played a role in the defection.[37] Whereas the US press did not make light of Sickles' extramarital affairs during his trial for killing Key, the general as a member of the Union army became fair game for Confederate propaganda attacks in 1861.

Although the Confederate press attacked the general for his previous indiscretions, many people in the North seemed to know about the events but did not appear critical of the general. One of these forgiving souls was the president. A possible reason for the president's feelings stemmed from Sickles' status as a political appointee with connections that may have proved useful to the president. In July 1864, President Abraham Lincoln visited the headquarters of the Army of the Potomac just prior to another campaign. After the various officers, including Sickles, presented themselves to the president, their wives, who were spending a few moments with their husbands before the campaign, also introduced themselves to Lincoln. The wife of Colonel Felix zu Salm-Salm, Princess Salm-Salm, asked Sickles: "General, he is a dear, good man, we want to kiss him; would it do any harm?" With Sickles' reply of "Not a bit of harm," the princess and some of the other ladies eagerly encircled and kissed Lincoln.[38] Mary Todd Lincoln reportedly admonished her husband and said that Sickles was lucky she was not present when he gave permission for the ladies to kiss the president.[39]

In an attempt to settle the ill feelings of his wife, Lincoln invited Sickles to dinner the next evening. After several attempts to lighten the mood of his wife, Lincoln made one final attempt. He turned to Sickles and said: "I never knew until last night that you were a very pious man." Confused by the remark, Sickles replied that Lincoln surely must have been misled. "'Not at all,' said the President, with simulated gravity. 'Mother says you are the greatest Psalmist in the army. She says that you are more than a Psalmist, you are a Salm-Salmist.'" Unable to contain herself, Mary laughed with the rest of the guests and ultimately forgave Sickles.[40] Although many people, including Mary, did not approve of Sickles' allegedly immoral lifestyle, his charm and good humor allowed him to win over many of those who disapproved. The reluctance of the prosecution and the public to bring up Sickles' past indiscretions captured the idea that it was acceptable, and at times, necessary for men to have sexual relations outside of marriage. Sickles obviously wanted to have his affairs, both long and short term—he saw Fanny White romantically for a number of years—yet Teresa was to remain faithful. Though most men seemingly did not engage in such behavior, a number of prominent men of the era did.

Another Union general, Judson Kilpatrick, made no attempts to keep his extramarital antics quiet. Kilpatrick became famous for his exploits with women. The young cavalry officer had even earned a notorious reputation during his years at West Point for womanizing. Like Sickles, Kilpatrick continued to keep numerous women on the side even after marrying his wife Alice.[41] "Kilpatrick often kept a girl in his quarters to perform 'sack duty and horizontal drill," according to an acquaintance. To his credit, however, Kilpatrick did not let race affect his choice in female companions. Kilpatrick had white, African American, "and even a Chinese girl" as female companions.[42]

Major General Judson Kilpatrick. Kilpatrick was a notorious womanizer that frequently brought prostitutes to his tent in camp.

In 1863, Kilpatrick made the acquaintance of one of the most famous prostitutes of the Civil War, Annie Jones. After returning from a visit to his wife and infant son during the last week of July, Kilpatrick met Jones when he rejoined his unit occupying positions near Fredericksburg. "Kilpatrick was so thrilled with Annie, he 'forgot' about his wife and baby son at West Point and invited her to share his tent."[43] The general became so enamored with Jones that he gave her wide latitude, seemingly allowing her to behave in any fashion that she wished. While in camp, Jones periodically dressed as a major and roamed the area on one of Kilpatrick's horses.[44]

After rooming with Kilpatrick for a period of time, Jones evidently became attracted by another, more dashing cavalry officer. When Kilpatrick left camp for three days on a raid, Jones moved her belongings into George Armstrong Custer's tent. Quickly, the news spread throughout the entire army. It was "embarrassing enough when the rejection was by a good woman, a disaster from a prostitute."[45] The move incensed Kilpatrick, who then had Jones arrested as a spy and sent to the Old Capital Prison in Washington, D.C.[46] In Jones' confession, she recounted in part the result of Kilpatrick's jealousy:

> While in the various camps I was furnished by the commanding officers with a tent and sometimes occupied quarters with the officers. . . . In the fall of 1862 I went to the Army of the Potomac. . . . General Kilpatrick became very jealous because of General Custer's attentions to me and went to General Meade's headquarters and charged me with being a Rebel spy. . . . I spent two and a half years in the Union army. . . . I invariably wore a major's stripes. . . . I was employed as a private friend or companion. . . . I have led a very roving, and, it may be, questionable, life.[47]

Ever a woman on the make, Jones' rumored involvement with a guard at the prison led to his dismissal.

Ultimately, Custer denied any romantic involvement with Jones, though he admitted that she "visited camp twice," but she did not sleep in his tent. Custer also denied any validity of her statement regarding himself and Kilpatrick.[48] Whether Custer had relations with Jones or not, his actions in denying a relationship certainly stemmed from his courtship of Elizabeth "Libbie" Bacon. The couple met in 1862 and married in 1864 when her father finally relented on Custer's promotion to brevet brigadier general. Most assuredly, knowing that Elizabeth's father would not allow her to marry a man who consorted with prostitutes while he was courting his daughter, George denied the accusations.

Although the common version of events held that Jones moved into Custer's tent, Custer's wife dismissed the charges of immorality against her husband.

> Of course with my husband's success and rapid promotion, the usual swarm of enemies presented him with maligning and falsehoods, and there were deprecations of his ability, which he tossed aside with the buoyancy [of] his temperament and repeating over of his watch words, 'Be sure you're right, then go ahead.' But it was no use. It is something few wives conquer.[49]

Brevet Major General George Armstrong Custer. Although Custer is not widely known for consorting with prostitutes, he did have an alleged tryst with a prostitute named Annie Jones.

Libbie mainly directed these words at Kilpatrick. In the following paragraphs she went on to describe Kilpatrick as a self-aggrandizing liar.[50] Although Libbie rejected what she believed to be slanderous rumors, she too had a bias. As Custer's loyal wife, and as a popular attraction on the lecture circuit after her husband's death, Libbie coveted and defended Custer's reputation as her most prized possession.

Following his tryst with Jones, Kilpatrick went on to have relations with other women. A disputed event occurred in November 1864 near Waynesborough, Georgia. During the night, a Confederate cavalry unit attacked Kilpatrick's encampment. The attack caught the Union soldiers unaware, and Kilpatrick reputedly fled in only a nightshirt. The Confederates claimed that the general had an African American prostitute in his tent just before the attack, which explained Kilpatrick's state of undress. Kilpatrick's men countered that their officer was tending to one of his horses just before the attack and did not have time to return to his tent for the rest of his clothes before fleeing. Several historians, including Kilpatrick's biographer, argue that the raid very likely caught Kilpatrick with a prostitute, but out of loyalty, his men simply defended the reputation of their "debauching commander."[51]

Ironically, the most famous event involving an officer and the subject of prostitution during the Civil War did not actually involve any prostitutes. As a part of General Winfield Scott's Anaconda Plan, segments of the Union army and navy successfully captured the city of New Orleans in April 1862. Military planners saw the goal of this operation as occupying the port, thereby cutting off access to much of the Mississippi River for Confederate traffic. Militarily, the Union forces accomplished the capture and occupation with relative ease because most of the Confederate defenders of the city had moved off previously to challenge Ulysses S. Grant in Tennessee.

The women of New Orleans did not submit to the wishes of General Benjamin Butler so easily. During the early days of the occupation, women spat or even flashed their under-garments at passing soldiers.[52] In several instances, wom-en actually dumped their full chamber pots on the heads of passing soldiers from their sec-ond-floor balconies.

At this point, Butler could not simply let the problematic women of New Orleans

Major General Benjamin Butler. Butler published General Orders No. 28 proclaiming that any women found insulting or harassing a Union soldier would be treated as a prostitute. Although that treatment was never discussed, the women of New Orleans quickly refrained from insulting soldiers.

continue to harass and demean his men unmolested. His problem of bringing the behavior to a stop proved exceptionally complex. The hanging of William Mumford quickly quelled any further intentions that the men of New Orleans had of making trouble for the occupation force. The same could not be done to the women to bring them under control. Although some of the women of the city departed from their accepted gender roles by spitting, flashing, and even dumping chamber pots on

Union soldiers, Butler and his command would have to act strictly within those gender roles in dealing with these women. If Butler acted too harshly, he might inadvertently spark further resistance from the male population coming to the defense of Southern womanhood.[53] According to historian Drew Gilpin Faust, many of the women who acted out proved "socially prominent, the kind of individuals who would attract both attention and sympathy if harsh measures turned them into martyrs." Butler refused to be "manipulated by women's simultaneous use and abuse of their femininity."[54] An arrest though, would lead to further notoriety for the women and, in addition to the male uprising, might foment more women to follow the example of the original dissenters. Butler understood that he needed an order that "would execute itself." According to Butler, "otherwise it would stir up more strife in its execution by the police than it would quell."[55] Alternatively, doing nothing turned out to have an unfortunate outcome as well. For a short period of time, Butler believed that the behavior would simply "die out" once the civilians experienced the even-handed treatment by the federal soldiers. His hopeful beliefs did not come to fruition.

The ultimate insult came as Flag Officer David Farragut and Colonel Henry Deming strolled to dinner. Butler stated, "there fell upon them what they first took to be a sudden and heavy shower." In a disgusting revelation, the two realized they were not soaked by a sudden evening thunderstorm, but the contents of a full chamber pot.[56]

In responding to these attacks by the women of New Orleans, Butler took carefully measured and surprisingly creative action. On May 15, 1862, he issued General Orders 28. The orders stated:

> As the officers and soldiers of the United States have been subject to repeated insults from the women (calling themselves ladies) of New Orleans in return for the most scrupulous non-interference and courtesy on our part, it is ordered that hereafter when any female shall by word, gesture, or movement insult or show contempt for any officer or soldier of the United States she shall be regarded and held liable to be treated as a woman of the town plying her avocation.[57]

Butler's orders, in fairly clear terms, stated that any women who continued to insult Union soldiers would be treated as prostitutes. Authorities understood that if they happened on offending women, they would arrest the women, hold them overnight in the "calaboose," and fine them five dollars the next morning.[58] Prior to the order, various staff officers expressed concerns about the interpretation of the order. Chief of Staff George Strong voiced distress over the wording. Strong said to Butler, "This order may be misunderstood, general. It would be a great scandal if only one man should act upon it in the wrong way." Butler alleviated Strong's concerns by retorting, "Let us then have one case of aggression on our side. I shall know how to deal with that case, so that it will never be repeated."[59]

Secretary of War William Seward even voiced concern about the order. He, like Strong, believed that a soldier might interpret the order as giving permission to rape offending women because the commander considered them prostitutes.[60] It is doubtful that Butler would have allowed the rape of women, however, even if they presented themselves openly as prostitutes. Prior to the order's actual publication, a Union soldier named Paddy Bassady insulted several ladies along Canal Street on the evening of May 15. The Second District Police took Bassady into custody and turned him over to the Provost Marshal. By their actions, the local authorities seemingly had assurances that, although the Union forces occupied the city, they would still be held to the standards of polite society.[61]

Butler and his staff deliberated over the exact phrasing of the orders. According to James Parton, Butler said during a discussion of the orders:

> Here we are conquerors in a conquered city; we have respected every right, tried every means of conciliation, complied with every reasonable desire; and yet we can not walk the streets without being outraged and spit upon by green girls. I do not fear the troops; but if aggression must be, let it not be all against us.[62]

Parton went on to argue that even if the general overtly permitted his troops to "outrage and ravish every woman who insulted them," the

Union soldiers would not have done so.[63] Whether they would have acted out or not, after the editor printed the order in the *Picayune* on May 17, the women discontinued their outrageous behavior. Although the editor placed General Orders No. 28 on the second page of the *Picayune*— just as he did every other order—the city took immediate and passionate notice of the typed lines.[64]

In the following weeks, other criminal offences appeared the *Picayune* with the noticeable absence of any references to women using extreme measures to express their disapproval of the federal presence.[65] They continued subtle rebellious action, however; some women of the city placed flower arrangements in their windows. Unbeknownst to the occupying forces, the arrangements contained a state flower from each of the Confederate states. More importantly, however, instances of spitting, cursing, and emptying chamber pots on soldiers ceased.[66]

Butler later wrote:

> The order executed itself. No arrests were ever made under it or because of it. All the ladies in New Orleans forbore to insult our troops because they didn't want to be deemed common women, and all the common women forbore to insult our troops because they wanted to be deemed ladies and these two classes were all the women secessionists of the city.

By May, the editor of the *Picayune* still had not reported on any misbehavior by the women or the city, nor would he in the months to come. Rumblings did emanate from other locations within the Confederacy, however, because of the implication that Butler considered the ladies who previously had committed such offenses to be acting like prostitutes as well. Southern editors became rabid over the news that a Yankee general insulted Southern womanhood in his words to the women of New Orleans. Various editors around the South spewed venom at Butler through their editorials. Some even went so far as to offer a reward for the capture or death of Butler.[67]

Butler's order incensed President Jefferson Davis. The Confederate president issued a lengthy proclamation describing the numerous "crimes" committed by Butler and his men in New Orleans. Chief among the crimes, he listed the charge that "the soldiers of the United States have been invited and encouraged by general orders to insult and outrage the wives, the mothers, and the sisters of our citizens."[68] Davis went on to declare:

> Benjamin F. Butler to be a felon, deserving of capital punishment. I do order that he be no longer considered or treated simply as a public enemy of the Confederate States of America, but as an outlaw and common enemy of mankind, and that in the event of his capture the officer in command of the capturing force do cause him to be immediately executed by hanging, and I do further order that no commissioned officer of the United States taken captive shall be released on parole before exchange until the said Butler shall have met with due punishment for his crimes.[69]

Reactions to the order centered on the dependence of women and their accepted role in Southern society. Faust argued that viewing Butler's order as an attack on Southern womanhood, allowed those opposing the order to claim that women could not be held accountable for their actions. Because the order depended on the behavior of the women of New Orleans, Butler charged that they had the power to determine their own status. Ultimately, with Order Number 28, "Butler acknowledged women as politically powerful."[70]

Butler's later orders did not receive attention on the scale of Number 28, even when they regarded women of the city. In one set of orders published in May 1862, following a prohibition for the observance of Jefferson Davis' fast day, the general issued another order concerning women. In his order, Butler directed "imprisonment in the calaboose, women of the town found on the street after nightfall."[71] Since Butler targeted only actual prostitutes with this order, no outcry surfaced—except from the prostitutes themselves possibly, but it was not recorded if indeed they spoke out.

Not everyone in the South, or in New Orleans for that matter, disagreed with the order. The editor at the *Picayune* argued that he could not hope for a more favorable outcome. Admittedly, the editor of the newspaper faced censorship by the Union forces. In an earlier edition prior to the release of General Orders 28, however, he commented on the sad behavior of the women of the city in regard to the federal soldiers.[72]

Ironically, the women who should have been the most insulted by the debacle, the prostitutes of New Orleans, seemed to take the event in stride and even with a bit of humor. As the higher classed women of the city could no longer fling waste on soldiers from their chamber pots, prostitutes pasted pictures of General Butler to the insides of their chamber pots.[73]

In addition to the apparent results brought about by General Orders No. 28, Butler's decision also had curiously unforeseen consequences. Following the widespread calls for Butler's head for insulting the women of New Orleans by insinuations regarding their careers, mentions of actual prostitutes in other cities quickly disappeared from local newspapers. The *Daily Richmond Whig* ceased reporting on the hundreds of prostitutes that worked in the city. Though reports and rants concerning such women had provided a staple for the daily columns for the newspaper, mentions of prostitutes became noticeably absent from the paper after Butler's order. It is very likely that the editor of the *Whig* believed continued reports of widespread prostitution in Richmond would give credence to an assumption that Southern women possessed very low morals and took to the sex trade easily.

With the large size of the Confederate and Union officer corps, inevitably the groups attracted a wide variety of personalities and beliefs. Because neither the Union army nor Confederate army had an official policy addressing prostitution and other vices, commanders acted in what they believed to be the best interest of their men. As a result, both armies experienced a wide variety of policies regarding prostitution. Most commanders probably avoided the issue as long as soldiers fulfilled their military obligations. Commanders at Nashville and Memphis recognized that a great number of soldiers inevitably procured the services of prostitutes and attempted to make the sex trade as safe as possible for those involved. Other general officers objected to the trade in the interests of maintaining military strength and discipline within the army. McClellan opposed the issue on grounds of maintaining discipline as well as a possible firsthand knowledge of venereal disease. Of the general officers who opposed the trade, many objections stemmed from their religious backgrounds. Both Jackson and Polk had strong religious convictions and encouraged the same religious fervor and morality among their men. Yet such encouragement had a limited impact. Only the men under the direct supervision of religious officers like Jackson and Polk had to maintain the semblance of piousness. The masses of enlisted men had the benefit of numbers and anonymity, which enabled them to engage in perceived immoral activities. Finally, a relatively few general officers offered an almost open endorsement of the sex trade. The press and the general public knew of the proclivities of Sickles, Kilpatrick, and Hooker for prostitutes. The generals made no attempt to conceal their activities. Whatever their reasons for opposing, endorsing, or being indifferent to the sex trade, the policies of general officers affected many thousands of enlisted men and junior grade officers.

Although, for the most part, Butler's experience in New Orleans did not directly relate to actual prostitutes, it did capture an unspoken discomfort that people had with the subject. Prior to Butler's order, newspaper editors around the country parodied local prostitutes as a way of discussing the subject in a lighthearted, flippant way. When Butler's order threatened to blur the line between prostitutes and Southern ladies, the newspaper accounts of real prostitutes disappeared. Southern newspaper editors also did not want to give any credence to assumptions that might arise out of the order that Southern cities provided innumerable prostitutes.

Taken as a whole, the widely divergent sex trade policies of general officers on both sides clearly reflected social conflicts over the sex trade and other vices by the US public. Like ordinary soldiers, general officers largely acquired their morals and norms from their upbringing. The generals then passed along the morals of their communities, rigid or pragmatic, to the men under them, who then adopted the notions of morality or rebelled against them.

5

Saving Bodies and Souls

As soon as the Civil War began, Americans attempted to safeguard both the health and morality of the newly inducted soldiers. Army doctors attempted to treat the infections of wayward soldiers through a series of remedies that they wrongly believed to be beneficial. Physicians employed mercury-based treatments for several ailments and highly caustic solutions for others. Although the major venereal diseases of syphilis and gonorrhea could not be cured by the medical technology of the period, treatment for the symptoms of the diseases did exist, and doctors attended to them with varying degrees of success. As physicians treated the symptoms of venereal diseases, the US Sanitary Commission educated Union soldiers about a wide variety of threats to their health, including venereal diseases. Venereal diseases became a serious concern among both armies. Just as the medical establishment looked to the physical implications of prostitution and venereal diseases, Civil War–era reformers sought to safeguard the spiritual well-being of soldiers. During the war, several agencies formed with this purpose in mind. The US Christian Commission provided soldiers with religious materials and alternative wholesome activities to divert them from gambling and drinking establishments, as well as the corruptions of pornography and prostitutes. The YMCA expanded its role during the war. Originally founded to provide a haven for "moral" men moving to the cities and away from home, the YMCA undertook a similar mission with the millions of young men that joined the armies of the Civil War. During the war, a wide variety of dissimilar groups sought to deter soldiers from consorting with prostitutes or to minimize the deleterious effects of diseases contracted from sex workers.

The fledgling state of medical knowledge during the mid-nineteenth century allowed venereal ailments and other diseases to persist, or at times even worsen because of medical intervention. In 1860, the medical establishment first began to consider germ theory, which posited germs as the agents of infections. The theory would not be fully adopted until almost fifteen years later. Until then, physicians employed an assortment of methods for treating diseases. Although not a favored form of treatment in 1860, a very small number of medical professionals still practiced bleeding as a curative measure.[1] Many soldiers during the war faced infection with malaria. Prior to the modern explanation for transmission, most people of the nineteenth century believed malaria traveled on the wind from marshy or swampy areas. The doctor at Fort Buchanan in New Mexico believed the soldiers in the fort remained uninfected because of a "small knoll, which acted as a kind of screen to shelter them from the carrying influence of the southwest wind."[2] Physicians also believed that the winds, rather than mosquitoes, carried yellow fever. To fend off possible outbreaks, authorities often quarantined ships offshore with infected sailors. Unknown to local doctors and the public, mosquitoes simply transmitted the infection by biting the sailors and then flying ashore for a later meal. Insects did not prove to be the only culprit in the spread of disease. The complete lack of sterilization also played a major role. Many times, the inspection of wounds introduced additional bacteria and viruses into the victim. The procedure for removing an arrow did not take cross-infection into account. The "surgeon pushed his finger into the wound along the arrow shaft. He then snaked a long forceps along his guarding finger and took a strong chase upon the embedded point," without washing his hands or the forceps before the procedure.[3] Similar methods for removing bullets in the Civil War led to comparable problems.

A few medicines actually performed according to their intended purposes. Quinine successfully fended off malaria if taken in sufficient doses.[4] More often than not, medical procedures and medicines provided, at most, a form of hope to the stricken. In itself, the presence of hope may or may not have forestalled aggressive diseases and may have even bolstered the body's immune system, though it did little else. In addition to medical doctors, advertisers in newspapers offered convoluted knowledge of effective treatments by hawking everything from "water cures" to "electrical" treatments.[5] Water cure promoters claimed that patients with venereal disease would "undergo a course of purification, not of swallowing 'drugs and dye-stuffs,' but by means of a rigid dietary, fresh air, simple exercise, and abundant bathing."[6] Because electricity remained very much a novelty during the period, healers offered the hope that mild electrical stimulation could cure a multitude of ailments. Dr. Worster advertised his "electrical baths" in Washington newspapers making claims such as "every species of disease is more successfully treated than results from the old practice."[7] "Electropathic Physicians" P. and W. B. Shedd proclaimed an "unerring system" of diagnosis in the same newspapers. The Shedds marketed to women, perhaps including prostitutes, claiming "we would say to the ladies especially that the various and complicated diseases particular to their sex readily yield to this sovereign agency, as thousands can testify who have tried its virtues."[8] Such remedies were not restricted to the North. Southerners found themselves bombarded with questionable cures from advertisers in their newspapers. On March 28, 1861, *The Memphis Daily Appeal* included two advertisements in the paper centered on "private diseases." Holloway's Pills and Ointment for "Domestic Remedies" sold alongside the famed "Cherokee Cure!" which treated venereal diseases as well as "nocturnal emissions and all diseases caused by deviating from the path of nature, and indulging in Self-Pollution."[9] Medical practitioners applied "chemical salves to sores or blisters that appeared on the skin; mercury nitrate of silver, or iodide of potassium cauterized the lesions."[10] Oliver Wendell Holmes "claimed that if all the medications in America were thrown into the sea, it would be better for Americans and worse for the fish."[11] Such was the state of medical knowledge at the opening of the Civil War, and as a result, soldiers routinely endured treatments that not only did little to alleviate their symptoms, but regularly added to their woes.

Syphilis emerged as one of the main venereal concerns that faced the medical departments of both sides. Once the disease infected the body, a small chancre developed in the genital region and often healed after a couple of weeks. Physicians referred to this as "primary syphilis." Following the initial symptom of a chancre, syphilis usually exhibited a rash called "secondary syphilis." The chancre of primary syphilis usually erupted within a week to three months after contracting the disease, with secondary syphilis following one to six months later. Once the rash subsided, the disease then moved into the tertiary stage. Symptoms from this stage quietly exhibited themselves from one year up to ten years after initial contact.[12] Tertiary syphilis resulted in serious health issues, sometimes leading to heart failure, dementia, atrophy of the brain, and death.[13] Tertiary syphilis typically did not produce symptoms that obviously linked it to the original disease, which resulted in many doctors diagnosing the patient as cured following the healing of the chancre or the rash in the secondary stage.

Dr. Freeman J. Bumstead, writing for the US Sanitary Commission, argued that "the most effective treatment consists in the destruction of the local sore [the initial chancre] by means of a powerful caustic. . . . Fuming nitric acid is the most convenient agent, and, if the fall of the eschar fails to leave a healthy surface, the application should be repeated."[14] Bumstead went on to claim "the administration of mercury for the primary sore may retard or altogether prevent the appearance of general symptoms."[15] Yet Bumstead and many other physicians of the period believed that most chancres ultimately did not prove to be syphilis. If the attending doctor thought the chancre did not seem to be syphilis, Bumstead recommended against using mercury as a treatment. "We are not justified in subjecting a patient to a mercurial course unless the necessity of it is apparent." Even in the 1860s, doctors recognized the dangers of prescribing mercury to patients and observed the young men closely during use of the element. If the patient reported lack of appetite, lethargy, or depression, "the administration of mercurials should be suspended, and afterward resumed, if necessary to complete the cure."[16] Bumstead went on to say "the action of mercury upon the bowels should, if necessary, be restrained by the addition of opium or astringents; and, in some instances, the internal use of the remedy must be suspended and inunction [sic] employed."[17]

Mercury proved to be such a harsh remedy that Bumstead cautioned "the treatment of syphilis should invariably be conducted in a hospital. The dangers to be apprehended from exposure and hardship, while pursing a mercurial course, are too great to admit this treatment being undertaken in camp."[18] In an introduction to the section on venereal diseases, *The Medical and Surgical History of the Civil War* echoed Bumstead's recommendations, but departed from his advice concerning restricting treatment to hospitals. According to *The Medical and Surgical History*, "treatment as a rule was first restricted to the local lesions, mercury or iodide of potassium being withheld until the development of secondary symptoms. No reference is made to scorbutic complications or to untoward results in constitutions undermined by the hardships of military service. In fact, a similar series of cases might easily have been gathered during the same period in the wards of our civil hospitals."[19] Surgeon J. G. Brandt wrote from New Orleans that syphilitic "sores yield readily to cauterization with acid nitrate of mercury and applications of black wash. . . . Sufficient time has not yet elapsed whether secondary symptoms will be developed."[20] Surgeon Ezra Read concocted one of the most harmful applications of mercury for his patients. Read argued: "for many years I have pursued the method of treatment by mercurial fumigation, which deposits the mercury upon the surface of the skin . . . induced by the heated vapor of water surrounding the patient in a close and air-tight bath."[21] Read's method of introducing mercury to the patient's system indeed proved the most effective because more mercury accumulated in the brain with this than with any other method of mercury absorption. Accumulations of the element resulted in tremors, disruptions in hearing and sight, and permanent damage to the brain and kidneys.[22] Fortunately, some surgeons began to drift away from the internal application of mercury. Surgeon Brandt in New Orleans wrote in his report: "I do not consider mercurials essential to the cure of the form of syphilitic ulcer most common in this city."[23] Sadly, offering mercury for the treatment or relief of syphilis symptoms did absolutely nothing but introduce additional suffering for the patient.

Though horrific, the treatment for orchitis did not involve poisonous elements. Nineteenth-century physicians recognized orchitis as an infection that resulted in the swelling of one or both testicles. Some sexually transmitted diseases, as well as the mumps, could result in orchitis.[24] For this disorder, Dr. Bumstead advocated applying leeches "just below the external abdominal ring, or bleeding from the scrotal veins."[25] Apparently, this condition did not present itself often because it is not enumerated alongside the statistics for syphilis and gonorrhea.

Civil War surgeons greatly concerned themselves with cases of gonorrhea. More than 109,000 Union soldiers contracted gonorrhea during the war. Although women frequently displayed few symptoms with the disease, most men suffered from an extreme burning during urination approximately three to five days after the initial infection. In prior years, doctors believed that gonorrhea and syphilis stemmed from the same infection. During the war, doctors like Bumstead dismissed the link. "The idea that gonorrhea is dependent upon the syphilitic virus, and requires the use of mercurials, is without foundation."[26] The practiced cures for the disease remained wide ranging. The variety of remedies included concoctions made from poke roots or berries, elder, wild sarsaparilla, sassafras, or prickly ash. A cure promoted by one Confederate Army surgeon claimed that "silk weed root put in whiskey and drank, given at the same time, pills of rosin from the pine tree, with very small pieces of blue vitrol would cure stubborn cases of gonorrhea."[27] Surgeon A. F. Peck of the 1st New Mexico Cavalry suggested a "saline cathartic" as a promising treatment. Assistant Surgeon P. W. Randall of the 1st California Infantry promoted the standard treatment for the disease: "urethral injections of nitrate of silver."[28] Dr. Bumstead concurred stating: "The 'abortive treatment' of gonorrhea is adapted only to the commencement of the disease, before acute symptoms have set in.

The best formula for its administration is a weak solution of nitrate of silver . . . injected every two hours until the discharge becomes thin and watery, (which usually takes place within twenty-four hours), and then omitted . . . abscesses along the course of the urethra should be opened as soon as detected, even before fluctuation can be felt." The treatment often continued for ten days.[29] The highly caustic nature of silver nitrate solution surely added immeasurable pain to the treatment experience.

Treatment with silver nitrate through a urethral injection had some interesting consequences. Physicians using this treatment claimed that the solution cured the infection. Although they believed that the infection had subsided, the treatment merely alleviated the symptoms of the disease. The silver nitrate actually killed the nerve endings of the urethra and eliminated the "burning sensation" of the bacteria attacking the mucosal membranes. Because the patient no longer suffered from any symptoms, the medical professionals of the period considered them to be cured.[30] Unfortunately, as a consequence of being pronounced cured, many former patients returned home after the war to unwittingly transmit gonorrhea to their wives or girlfriends. During the war, "cured" men also participated in furthering the epidemic of venereal diseases by infecting healthy prostitutes, who in turn infected other men.

Although physicians and the military worked at safeguarding the physical health of the soldiers, other groups on both sides worked tirelessly to protect the souls of soldiers from being tainted by vice, including prostitution. The British and Foreign Bible Society formed to smuggle Bibles through the blockade to Confederate soldiers. Additional missionary societies formed to distribute Bibles, tracts, and other religious readings. The soldiers, often starved for reading materials, happily accepted any form of text. Perhaps partly because of this lack of intellectual stimulation, Christian groups achieved the goals of spreading their message. Even military officers took part in the religious work. Confederate General Thomas "Stonewall" Jackson charged that "each branch of the Christian Church should send into the army some of its most prominent ministers. . . . These ministers should give special attention to preaching to regiments which are without chaplains."[31]

As the war dragged on, a growing concern for the morality of the young men, the armies, and the country emerged. One soldier reported: "men that four months ago would not use a profane word can now out swear many others, and those who would even shun a checker board now play cards for profit." The same soldier went on to claim that the many "fast women" in Corinth, Mississippi, used cheap whiskey to demoralize many of the men there.[32]

At times, such religious pressure on the soldiers and officers became questionable. Not only did armies face demands to avoid vice, such as prostitutes, alcohol, and gambling, but religious leaders also occasionally cautioned military commanders against fighting on Sundays if possible. The editor of the *Daily National Intelligencer* even suggested that if General Irvin McDowell could have postponed the Battle of Bull Run for one day, fighting on Monday rather than Sunday, the outcome might have been much different.[33]

Religious authorities mounted a tremendous amount of pressure on Major General George McClellan in the fall of 1861, calling for "more respect for the Sabbath." The general succumbed to the effort and in September 1861 issued the following order:

> We are fighting in a holy cause and should endeavor to deserve the devine [sic] favor of the Creator. Unless in the case of an attack by the enemy or some other extreme military necessity, it is commended to commanding officers that all work shall be suspended on the Sabbath; that no unnecessary movements shall be made on that day; that the men shall, as far as possible, be permitted to rest from their labors; that they shall attend Divine service after the customary Sunday morning inspection, and that officers & men alike use their influence to insure the utmost decorum and quiet on that day. The General Commanding regards this as no idle form. One day's rest in seven is necessary to men and animals; more than this, the observance of the holy day of the God of Mercy & Battles is our sacred duty. George B. McClellan, Major General Commanding[34]

The editor of the *Daily National Intelligencer* praised McClellan's orders, claiming that the United States would prevail "not merely because we have the most men & the most money, but because we have the right on our side, & because we have hearts large enough & pure enough to feel it, & and wills to defend a holy cause."[35] For some Americans, morality as well as adherence to religious convictions would ensure victory. Apparently, many of the men under McClellan's command felt the same. The *Daily National Intelligencer* reported on the Monday following the first Sunday under McClellan's new order that the soldiers seemed to have obeyed his command. Camp remained fairly quiet with many of the local churches full.[36] Unfortunately, it proved impossible to determine how many of McClellan's men saw Sundays as a day of religious reflection and how many saw it as simply a welcome respite.

In addition to larger Christian groups seeking to secure a presence in the armies, smaller organizations emerged with a desire to cater to select groups of soldiers. The YMCA, famous for maintaining morality among new arrivals to the cities, formed the "Ironsides Regiment." The infantry unit advertised for 750 men with "moral character & habits, to be clean, abstain from alcohol, and not swear."[37] In April 1861, the YMCA also began distributing tracts to soldiers moving through New York City. One month later, in May, the organization formed the Army Committee to provide help for soldiers during the war and published *The Soldiers' Hymn Book*.[38] The association also published letters from members as a means of providing other men guidance. In one such letter Judge E. Rockwood Hoar wrote to his son Samuel advising him to keep in mind his upbringing. "Remember always your home & your friends— those who will welcome your return with pride & joy if you shall come back in virtue & honor; who will cherish your memory if, faithful & true, you have given up your life; but to whom your disgrace would cause a pang sharper than death."[39] Although most parents and friends would be happy to have relatives return from the war unscathed, regardless of their "questionable actions," some people resorted to drastic measures to warn soldiers away from such activities.

YMCA members saw spectacular activity within the organization in the opening months of the Civil War. At a meeting on the previous year's work, members claimed that the YMCA published 4,610 scriptures and other religious works for soldiers.[40] Later that year, at a meeting in New York, YMCA members began serious consideration of forming a "Christian Commission," which later became the US Christian Commission.[41] The US Christian Commission attempted to recruit ministers from the hometowns of various regiments. Members of the commission thought that the ministers would pass news of bad behavior back to the communities, as well as relate news of home, promoting the self-discipline that many young men exhibited in small town communities.[42] The commission also founded a lending library with the hopes of drawing attention away from "erotic materials typically available" to soldiers. The members had such political connections they successfully added a provision to the Postal Act of 1865 banning the shipment of erotica to soldiers.[43] Although they might have missed the ease of ordering erotica through the mail, many soldiers appreciated the other efforts of the Christian Commission. In a letter to his wife, Dr. John Bennitt said that the commission did "much good work in supplying those things that conduce to the physical and moral well being of the soldier."[44]

The YMCA and other religious groups did not operate solely in the North. Chapters sprang up in the South seeking to save the souls of soldiers. The Richmond members of the YMCA held open meetings calling on soldiers to attend and touting the meetings as "an opportunity of meeting with Christian brethren of Richmond."[45] Rev. H. C. Hornaday oversaw the conversions of many young soldiers in an Atlanta hospital. In May 1862, he wrote to the *Daily Richmond Whig*, "there have been quite a number of conversions in the hospitals, and I have conversed with many who are anxiously inquiring what they must do to be saved."[46]

To counter what some people saw as the exponential growth of vice, many newspaper editors and moralizing groups tried to reign in the behavior. On February 23, 1863, the editor of the *Daily Morning Chronicle* of Washington, D.C., announced a meeting of the US Christian Commission stating: "We should . . . endeavor to prevent our soldiers from thus becoming familiar with vice," so we can return to a

A US Christian Commission establishment in Richmond, Virginia. The Christian Commission provided moral as well as health assistance for Union soldiers during the war.

polite society after the war.[47] Another Washington newspaper, *The Daily National Intelligencer*, periodically announced "Daily Union Prayer Meetings" in the capital.[48]

As a whole, activism in philanthropic societies such as the YMCA spiked during the first year of the war and continued to operate at impressive levels for its duration. In an effort to assist soldiers, donations to military organizations rose substantially—sometimes to the detriment of civilian charities.[49] Civilians in the North and South worked to aid soldiers. Southerners faced the problem of supplying their soldiers with basic necessities. Groups organized hospital aid societies as well as "collected clothing, hospital stores, blankets, and other supplies the Confederate government could not furnish to its troops."[50] Ironically, the

Northern charities, at times, faced issues of too many incoming donations with conflicts erupting over the distribution of such goods.[51]

The US Sanitary Commission also surfaced as a group that looked to the physical well-being of soldiers and sailors. The Sanitary Commission frequently cooperated with the Christian Commission endeavoring to better the living conditions of military men. The initial impressions by the Sanitary Commission of the Union Army caused much concern. In his report on the commission during the war, Charles J. Stille wrote that "a loose impression prevailed that volunteers should not be controlled by the ordinary methods of military discipline."[52] Stille charged that the new recruits believed themselves to be immune to "those evils which had demoralized armies made up of different material in former wars." Such views led to a rise in disease that killed soldiers at a rate that would "exceed ten-fold those of the battle-field [sic]."[53] Stille summed up his feelings on the future of the green armies in the following lines

> To the calm observer who knew anything of history, the view of this mass of enthusiastic and undisciplined men, calling themselves soldiers suggested some sad forebodings. It constituted a precious element of the vital force of the population, and was composed precisely of that class of men who from their previous habits and modes of life were not only least likely to bear well exposure and privation, but also, certain to become victims of diseases which have always proved the scourge of armies.[54]

Because the Sanitary Commission's duty was to see to the overall health of the men, its attention focused on the most pressing problems. It did so by placing "sanitary or preventive service before relief." By preventing disease within the ranks, the commission hoped to retain the fighting strength of the army.[55]

When the Sanitary Commission came into being at the opening of the Civil War, the commissioners promoted a variety of reforms. Prior to the first Battle of Bull Run, the commission promoted an order "forbidding the bringing of liquor into camp, only to be told that such orders could not be enforced."[56] Other suggestions found a somewhat more accepting audience. The commission urged commanders to seek out fresh vegetables for their men in the prevention of scurvy, the rapid construction of hospitals to house sick and wounded soldiers, and the facilitation of an easy method for soldiers to transfer money to their families as a means of improving morale and settling concerns for families back home.[57] As the head of the commission, George Templeton Strong heartily advocated for improved care for soldiers and completely devoted himself to the work. He wrote in his diary: "I believe we are doing a considerable amount of service to the country and that we have saved more men than have been lost in any two days' fighting since the war began.[58]

When mentioning the Sanitary Commission in their memoirs, diaries, and letters, several physicians spoke of the commission's work in preventing scurvy and little else. They wrote enthusiastic praise for the members of the commission in their efforts. The Sanitary Commission also attempted to provide soldiers aid in attending to their physical well-being. Some medical doctors ultimately credited the Sanitary and Christian Commissions for reducing the effects of scurvy through their donations.[59]

The attention to scurvy by the Christian Commission as well as the Sanitary Commission provided a glimpse at a larger picture. Although both organizations endeavored to improve the lives of soldiers, the Christian Commission predominantly set out to attend to the spiritual needs and morality of the soldiers. Likewise, the US Sanitary Commission formed to augment the medical corps in keeping the soldiers physically healthy through education, supplementing diets, and preventive care.[60] Both groups set out with lofty and wide-reaching goals, but they focused their efforts on the most pressing needs. Thus, venereal diseases and general vice often slipped by unaddressed in the ever-mounting list of priorities for Civil War commanders and reformers.

In addition to simply treating cases of venereal infection, a few progressive military authorities attempted to stem the tide of disease while accepting the inevitability of the sex trade. The concept of controlling the spread of venereal disease while allowing the sex trade to continue occurred during the federal occupation of Nashville, Tennessee. Colonel George Spalding had a number of prostitutes sent to Louisville, Kentucky, by train shortly after the occupation. When the women quickly returned and others followed, he made a second attempt to remove prostitutes from the city by ordering Captain John Newcomb of the riverboat *Idahoe* to take the women north in 1863.[61] The catalyst for the second attempt came when a Lieutenant Brannon, of the provost guard, saw a carriage stop in front of a brothel. A cavalry officer exited the carriage, leaving the driver with a prostitute, and entered the brothel. Brannon immediately jumped into the carriage and ordered the driver to take them to the provost marshal's office. The provost marshal reprimanded the driver and prostitute, and then determined to "abate the nuisance."[62] No other city agreed to accept the riverboat full of prostitutes, so Newcomb brought the women back to Nashville.[63]

According to a Surgeon Robert Fletcher, "after the attempt to reduce disease by the forcible expulsion of the prostitutes had, as it always has, utterly failed, the more philosophic plan of recognizing and controlling an ineradicable evil has met with undoubted success." Fletcher referred to a system of licensing prostitutes, inspecting them for disease, and hospitalizing infected women. In his report Fletcher claimed:

> Among the difficulties to be overcome was the opposition of the public women. This has so effectively disappeared that I believe they are now earnest advocates of a system which protects their health and delivers them from quacks & charlatans. . . . They gladly exhibit to their visitors the 'certificate' when it is asked for, a demand, I am informed, not infrequently made. The majority of the patients in the hospital are not sent from the inspection room, but consist of women who, suspecting their malady, have voluntarily come for examination and treatment. . . . Under these regulations a marked improvement was speedily noticed in the manner and appearance of the women. When the inspections were first enforced many were exceedingly filthy in their persons and apparel and obscene and coarse in their language, but this soon gave place to cleanliness and propriety.[64]

Reports of the "systematized efforts at prevention" claimed the program was a rousting success. Surgeon W. M. Chambers, in charge of Hospital No. 15 at Nashville, recorded that out of the 994 cases of infected soldiers seen at his hospital, only 13 had picked up the disease in Nashville, with the remainder infected somewhere else. After twelve months of the program, around one-third of the estimated six to seven hundred prostitutes in Nashville carried licenses. Army surgeons attributed the falling number of infected prostitutes to an assumption "that many diseased cortesans left the city on the publication of the order rather than be subjected to hospital treatment." Nearly a year after the Nashville program began, L. L. Coxe "an inspector or agent of the US Sanitary Commission, proposed the plan from Nashville for Memphis." Coxe studied the system in Nashville and then returned to Memphis. On August 26, 1864, he delivered his report to the commanding general of the department, who in turn ordered Colonel Thomas H. Harris—the Assistant Adjutant General and Mayor of Memphis—to implement the system. Five days later, on August 31, the city of Memphis began a program of licensing prostitutes.[65]

Prior to mustering out of the military, each soldier in the regiment submitted to a final medical examination conducted by the regimental surgeon. The surgeon documented the presence of any injuries or diseases, including venereal diseases. The doctors conducted this "Medical examination of men for military service and frauds to be guarded against." While gaining a realization that many young men purchased sex from prostitutes and risked disease, the US Army also attempted to reduce the number of fraudulent claims by men who contracted venereal diseases after they mustered out of the military.

With so many soldiers contracting venereal diseases that threatened to hinder the efforts of the military, several groups emerged or expanded their roles in attempts to control the epidemic. Although their primary goal centered on keeping soldiers away from prostitutes, the groups went about their work in different ways: either trying to prevent disease or vice in general. Regimental surgeons attempted to cure gonorrhea, syphilis, and orchitis using silver nitrate, mercury, leeches, or even bleeding. Although leeches and bleeding patients did not have any positive effect, they usually did not have a negative impact either. Mercury and silver nitrate treatments often misled the patient into believing that they had obtained a cure. The belief unfortunately resulted in the soldiers later suffering from the disease in the case of syphilis and passing both diseases on to future sexual partners. Not only did soldiers seek the assistance of military surgeons in treating venereal diseases, but they also procured treatments from civilians. Usually advertised in newspapers and lacking any oversight, civilian cures remained ineffective and often contained ingredients such as opium or other toxins. In a time of mostly negatives for medical policy, one positive stemmed from efforts of dealing with venereal diseases during the war. The lack of a formal policy or regulation by either army allowed the experimental programs at Nashville and Memphis to take place. Surgeons and provost guards in the two cities worked together to isolate soldiers and prostitutes with either syphilis or gonorrhea. Though the actual success of the program remains in question, the growing acceptance of the reality that men sought out prostitutes, followed by the efforts to regulate those conditions, became important. The US military has waivered in its stance on this issue since the Civil War. During World War I, the US Army prohibited visits to brothels. World War II saw a grudging acceptance and efforts to protect the soldiers through education and treatment with antibiotics. Finally, the US Army actually regulated at least one brothel during the Vietnam War with the intention of limiting exposure to disease; a weekly dose of penicillin for all of the sex workers attended to that aspect of the operation.[66]

Reformers also attempted to deter soldiers from visiting prostitutes. The YMCA used peer pressure to limit their members from visiting prostitutes, gambling, drinking alcohol, and other vices. The US Christian Commission held prayer meetings and pushed legislation through Congress that prohibited sending pornography to soldiers. The US Sanitary Commission likewise attempted to keep soldiers away from prostitutes, in the name of maintaining the health of the soldiers. Faced with attending to the needs of hundreds of thousands of soldiers, some of the organizations found these goals less pressing than other key issues such as scurvy.

6

Capitals, Armies, and Refugees: Washington and Richmond

During the Civil War era, neither side developed a military-wide policy with regard to prostitution. As a result, various localities evolved their own methods of addressing prostitution and venereal diseases. Many cities simply continued existing policies regarding the sex trade. Larger inland cities as well as port cities and commercial hubs often maintained their previous methods of dealing with the institution. Such policies frequently consisted of allowing prostitutes to conduct business if they remained discreet. Local judges fined sex workers in the event that they caused a significant disturbance whether on a public street or in the confines of a brothel. Authorities in other cities, such as the training areas around Cairo, Illinois, seemingly resolved to accept that nothing could be done about the prostitutes who catered to the men streaming through the training camps.[1] The training camps at Cairo saw hundreds of prostitutes and multitudes of intoxicated soldiers milling about in such numbers that authorities could do little to control the situation. Military authorities in a few areas went to the opposite extreme, attempting to completely prohibit soldiers from participating in the sex trade during the war. Although most large cities in the United States at least tolerated prostitution in select areas prior to the war, a few cities attempted to completely shut down areas of prostitution as a means of keeping soldiers away from the sex trade altogether. This chapter will examine two cities, Washington, D.C., and Richmond, Virginia, and their policies on the issue. Both cities served as the capitals of their respective governments. In the early months of the war, police and provost guards attempted to ban all soldiers from visiting brothels in Washington, D.C. In contrast, Richmond had a longtime relationship with prostitution. As long as the ladies maintained some decorum, authorities in Richmond maintained some control over the institution through the course of the war. Examinations of both Washington, with its early attempt at prohibition, and Richmond, with its more liberal view of the sex trade, reveal that both capitals experienced problems with prostitution that required the attention of authorities. No easy solution presented itself for the predicaments created when prostitutes and soldiers consorted with one another.

As military units gathered for training around the capitals of Washington and Richmond in the beginning months of the Civil War, the surrounding townspeople gushed with a romanticized view of the coming war. The desire to be a part of the war effort led many civilians to form soldiers' aid societies. Just as civilians in the North created aid societies such as the YMCA and the US Christian Commission, so too did the citizens of the Southern states. A group of Southern women in Richmond formed the Ladies Military Aid Society in July 1861 to help supply soldiers.[2] In November, another group, the Ladies Military Sewing Society, formed in Richmond with the aim of distributing uniforms.[3] From July through mid-November, the city of Richmond saw little change in the standard of living of its citizens. With the exception of increasing numbers of soldiers around the city, much remained the same. According to Ernest Furgurson, people gathered regularly at the training camps outside of Richmond to watch drills. Some local girls even developed "crushes on young men they had never met."[4] As the Confederate forces left to face the Union armies, "girls applauded troops passing in their bright peacetime uniforms."[5] For a very short while, it seemed that the people of Richmond believed the war would be brief and involve very little sacrifice on their part. Unfortunately for the Confederates in Richmond, the first winter of the war quickly prompted a slipping economy. Because many young men already had left for the war, incomes decreased, crops took longer to harvest, and untold monies went into providing soldiers with the accoutrements that families and the government believed they needed during their foray into northern Virginia. As the economy began to flounder, charities became the first to have problems. On December 9, 1861, the *Richmond Daily Whig* reported that the "Soldiers' Aid Society" already had exhausted all of its funds.[6] Surplus monies in Richmond quickly disappeared as inflation began to dominate the Confederate economy. As prices rose for essentials, such as food and shelter, the citizens of Richmond, as well as the soon-to-be arriving refugees, found aid societies in short supply, which forced the destitute to greater and greater lengths.[7]

Prostitution had maintained a long-standing presence in Richmond. According to historian Kenneth Radley, "Richmond could also lay claim to being the vice capital of the Confederacy."[8] The city's mayor tolerated prostitution as long as the sex workers did not cause problems.[9] The retention of money in the community of Richmond endured as a strong incentive to overlook the sex trade.[10] Initially, the prostitutes sequestered their businesses in certain sections of town or the local theater. Although many people of Richmond attempted to ignore the issue, the editor of the *Richmond Daily Whig* took great offense to their presence anywhere in the city. He remarked that the local theater—a common place for prostitutes to frequent—"is now in part, a place of assignation, and a rendezvous for all the disorderly elements of society which congregate there."[11] In December 1861, he happily reported what he considered to be progress in that establishment. The owner of the theater closed down all of the bars in his business. The editor gave no explanation, though he reported that, much to his chagrin, the third tier remained open and double entendre continued on the stage. He touted a "step in the right direction [after which the] theatre would again be popular with all classes excepting those of the baser sort."[12] During that winter, the theater burned down, but the owner quickly had the structure rebuilt. It appeared that this time, the owner chose to run a "moral" establishment and did not include areas for the sex trade. The editor replied to the news saying "it is pleasing to note the good order enforced in the house, and if this is continued, there will be little ground for fault finding."[13] Though the theater owner no longer promoted the sex trade, prostitutes found a plethora of other business locales.

Later, as more and more soldiers arrived in Richmond for training and reorganization, throngs of prostitutes flowed into the city. Many came as destitute refugees simply seeking to survive the war; others came with the intent of working in the sex trade catering to the soldiers in the surrounding areas. The increasing numbers of prostitutes proved too much for another Richmond editor. On May 13, 1862, the editor of the *Richmond Dispatch* railed that "shame-faced prostitutes of both sexes" offered their services in many areas of town.[14] The papers consistently reported on the state of morals in the community. Clara Coleman rode through respectable areas of Richmond in her carriage "making mouths at the ladies & bowing & kissing & flirting her hand at military officers."[15] In mid-1862, the ladies of the evening continued openly mocking polite society and intruding into "their" sections of town. At that time, a madam opened a brothel directly across the street from the YMCA hospital for soldiers. The hospital staff complained that the women delayed the recovery of their patients by suggestively beckoning to the convalescing soldiers to leave their sick beds and visit the brothel.[16]

Through newspaper exchanges, the editor of the *Daily Mississippian* remarked in April 1863 that Richmond again faced a downward economic spiral. Not anticipating the costs of living in wartime Richmond, many women went to the city "penniless, helpless, unadvised, unrestrained by the presence of those to whom they are known, they resort to means of securing assistance of which at home they would never have dreamed."[17] For the most part, prostitutes in Richmond seemed to have arrived without the intention of entering the sex trade, but rather to seek assistance in surviving the war. Upon seeing so many other refugees in the same situation, many women turned to prostitution as a means of survival. The editor of the *Richmond Daily Whig* seemed to believe in such a scenario and periodically printed stories corroborating the image. On April 30, 1864, he printed the story of "Miss D. Bayne." The young lady apparently came to Richmond to visit her brothers in the army. She arrived absolutely destitute and lived in the streets during her stay. In the Mayor's Court, attendees took up a collection for the girl to pay for her return to Tuscaloosa, Alabama. The editor did not mention whether Bayne worked as a prostitute, however, most citizens did not simply drop by the Mayor's Court for a visit.[18]

The struggle with morality in Washington, D.C., somewhat mirrored that of Richmond. Prior to the war, sexual commerce within the capital functioned in a fairly discreet manner. Politicians, wealthy men, and even working men occasionally sought out the company of sex workers. Solicitations occurred privately with hushed tones. Once the war began, however, a multitude of soldiers and other distractions allowed the sex trade to occur openly.[19] According to one war correspondent visiting in the capital in 1862, the city "was the most pestiferous hole since the days of Sodom and Gomorrah. The majority of the women on the streets were openly disreputable . . . in fact, every possible form of human vice and crime, dregs, offscourings and scum had flowed into the capital and made of it a national catch-basin of indescribable foulness."[20]

Also, as had occurred in Richmond, the civilian authorities seemed to accept prostitution's existence and realized that little could be done to end the trade. Newspaper reports abound concerning the institution in Washington. On February 23, 1863, authorities arrested eight women at Sarah Austin's brothel for "disorderly conduct." The court fined the women $2.94 and released them.[21] The relatively small fine supports the idea that the public tolerated prostitution as long as sex workers and their clients did not cause major disturbances. Authorities broke up a fight at Philomena Cook's brothel on the same night. Evidently the brothel had been the site of previous trouble because Superintendent William B. Webb reportedly took the keys to the house and would not allow it to be used as a brothel again.[22] One of the most troublesome situations in Washington involved the Light family. The mother served as the madam and allegedly forced the daughters to prostitute themselves. Whether the daughters entered into the sex trade of their own free will or not is impossible to know.[23] The Light family proved to be an inventive lot. They once hired an organ grinder with a monkey to perform at the brothel while the daughters supposedly stripped to the music. Unfortunately, the event attracted the police in addition to the customers "and they were carried, monkey and all before the magistrate."[24]

In late 1862, the provost marshal began keeping records of the numerous brothels in Washington. That year, an estimated 450 brothels operated throughout the capital with an estimate of five thousand prostitutes—both streetwalkers and brothel workers. The editor of *The Evening Star* newspaper downplayed the estimate, claiming that only about five hundred prostitutes resided in the capital prior to the war. According to Margaret Leech, in "New York, Philadelphia, and Baltimore, and even in Chicago and St. Louis, ambitious madams had closed their houses; and, shepherding a choice selection of their misses, had entrained for the Washington market."[25] Unlike many of the sex workers in Richmond, most of the prostitutes that gravitated to Washington, D.C., arrived with the full intention of selling sex. One of the highest estimates of the number of prostitutes in Washington claimed that fifteen thousand working women existed in the capital. Prostitutes occupied nearly every section of the city. Historian Ernest Furgurson claimed:

> freelancing women, white, black and mulatto, beckoned troops picketing or idling around the edges of outlying camps. Streetwalkers worked in alleys and parks of the city, and some entrepreneurs of a higher esthetic class set up in respectable neighborhoods. But the hotbed of vice in the wartime capital was within a few minutes stroll of the White House, the Treasury and Willard's Hotel.[26]

In an effort to get the sex trade as well as other vices under control, in 1861, General George McClellan appointed Colonel Andrew Porter as Provost Marshal of Washington. Porter enforced orders from McClellan that were meant to promote the health of the army through regulating morality. Among other actions, the provost guards cooperated with the police in raiding brothels, frequently arresting soldiers, enforcing the major's last call of 9:30 for "liquor houses," and closed gambling establishments.[27] At times, the two organizations seemed overly zealous in their efforts. In October 1861, McClellan ordered the provost guard to stop issuing passes for relatives to visit soldiers in camp because of the lack of discipline in the army.[28] The provost guard and police also increased the provost "sentinels" during the Christmas celebration. According to the *Daily National Intelligencer*, soldiers still had permission to celebrate the holiday, but the officers believed it prudent to provide additional oversight for the usual holiday ribaldry.[29]

Over the course of a year, however, Porter's health suffered from overwork. Porter's "sickness, contracted in the untiring discharge of his duties, compelled him to ask to be relieved from the position he had so ably and energetically filled."[30] Although Porter left the office, the practice of arresting soldiers inside brothels continued.

On January 9, 1863, weeks before Ambrose Burnside lost his position as commander of the Army of the Potomac, the order to arrest all soldiers in brothels expired. After that day, the provost guard only arrested soldiers accused of causing disturbances in brothels.[31] A number of factors likely led to this change in policy. Many soldiers visited prostitutes and brothels without causing any problems or breaking any other laws. Also, the commanders of the Army of the Potomac had a much more serious issue that required attention: the war. In Washington, D.C., prostitution simply became "accepted as a necessary evil."[32] That acceptance came with close scrutiny. As more soldiers openly visited the brothels, the provost guards made more visits to the establishments in an effort to keep things under control. Near the end of the war on April 1, 1865, the Provost Marshal General issued an order attempting to gain increased oversight. The order read: "All brothels and bawdy-houses will be visited as frequently as possible during the evening, and if found disorderly the inmates will be ordered to report at the Central Guard-House on the following morning, to be convicted by the testimony of the officer having command of the patrol."[33]

Though General Joseph Hooker often received credit for relaxing controls on prostitution in Washington during his tenure as commander of the Army of the Potomac, the decision to reevaluate the policy actually occurred just before Hooker took command. Accounts of Hooker's philandering with prostitutes no doubt gave rise to the belief that Hooker personally opened brothels to the soldiers of the Union army. Hooker did relocate many prostitutes to a central district in the capital. However, the general undertook this move in an effort to control the sex trade, realizing the impossibility of ending prostitution.[34]

Not only did the prostitutes of both cities cause quite a nuisance by openly offering their services to the soldiers, but the soldiers also did their part in creating cities of vice. Reports regularly appeared in the *Richmond Daily Whig* remarking about the problems with the soldiers in the city. Provost guards frequently arrested soldiers on charges of drunkenness and held them until their commanding officers retrieved the miscreants. By September 1861, the editor of the *Whig* had already grown tired of the ribaldry among soldiers, stating that "the evil should be abated."[35] Of all of the soldiers training around Richmond, the Louisiana Zouaves apparently excelled at being wilder than most of their comrades. The Zouaves "made hospitable Richmond think twice about its open doors."[36] After drills, one group of Zouaves went to Coleman's brothel. They reportedly shot out lights, broke furniture, and frightened the women away. They then found their way to the establishment of Lizzie Hubbard, who summoned the police. The Mayor's Court tried several of the men for raping one of the inmates at Coleman's brothel. Probably because her brothel had been the scene of previous incidents, the court charged Hubbard with "operating a disorderly house and ordered her to move out of the neighborhood."[37] The editor did not comment on the reason that Hubbard's brothel closed while Coleman's remained open, but Coleman may have operated a much more discreet and orderly house. Unfortunately, such violent events regularly appeared in the local newspaper.[38]

The soldiers in Washington, D.C., exhibited remarkably similar behavior with regard to vice. The issue of vice became a concern for the community very early in the war. The editor of the *Daily National*

Intelligencer encouraged officers to require their men to report directly to the McClellan's headquarters and "not allow their men to wander about & be subjected to arrest by the Provost Guard."[39] One of the major problems in Washington resulted from the lack of facilities to incarcerate prisoners. Criminals convicted in Washington had to be taken to Albany, New York, to serve time. The county jail in Washington fell into a terrible state of disrepair during the war and the federal government used the district penitentiary to store ammunition.[40] The military guard house could not even contain prisoners effectively. In September 1861, four soldiers escaped by breaking through a crumbling wall. Though the four quickly found themselves recaptured and in the city jail, it became obvious that only the most dangerous prisoners would have to be transported to Albany for secure incarceration.[41] Criminals committing regularly reported crimes such as stealing from the quartermaster's stores often did not face incarceration because of a lack of facilities in which to confine them.[42] Convicted soldiers faced a variety of punishments from simple fines, forfeiture of pay, hard labor, or even dismissal from service for more serious offenses.[43]

Enlisted soldiers did not have a monopoly on vice in the capital. Officers also found time to consort with prostitutes and attract the attention of the local press. The *Evening Star* reported that two uniformed officers "sat hugging and kissing their 'fair but frail' companions in full view of a regiment on full dress parade."[44] Another officer allegedly attended a show at the Odd Fellows Hall with a prostitute on each arm. The ultimate offense came in early 1862, when Pennsylvania Avenue began filling with prostitutes "promenading with officers or lolling in their carriages."[45] Even at that early date, it became obvious that the more pressing issues of the war allowed transgressions of relatively minor vice to be ignored by the authorities.

In addition to concerns with prostitution, both armies paid close attention to issues with alcohol. Because many bars and liquor houses doubled as impromptu brothels, controlling alcohol proved doubly beneficial. Authorities in Richmond also saw the prohibition of alcohol as a means of securing the food supply. Grain used in the production of alcohol unnecessarily reduced the amount of grain that could be consumed by an increasingly hungry public. Initially, the Virginia legislature passed a law forbidding the distillation of whiskey from grain, with no mention of "peach brandy or apple jack, the precious souls." The editor of the *Richmond Daily Whig* humorously noted that the move would open the market for Northern distillers because "all the military lines in creation can't blockade whiskey."[46] The law did not affect distillers in other states, and even led to increased production outside of Virginia. Some distillers in other states even advertised in Virginia newspapers seeking men to operate their distilleries.[47] Several Richmonders found increased profits in breaking the law and selling illegal whiskey. Restaurateurs and confectioners found themselves in the Mayor's Court occasionally for such crimes.[48] An estimate of "50-100 confectioneries about Richmond" sold candy as a front for a "bar room located in a back apartment." If the authorities shut one down, another simply opened elsewhere.[49] In May 1862, the editor of the *Richmond Daily Whig* printed General Orders No. 8 making illegal the production of wines, spirits and malt liquors. The order prohibited "distilling, selling, giving away, or in any manner disposing of such beverages." [50] Just as before, entrepreneurs attempted to circumvent the law. Ads appeared in the *Richmond Daily Whig* offering alcohol "for medical purposes."[51] Obtaining a prescription from a medical doctor seemed to be a relatively simple proposition in a time with extremely little oversight by any sort of medical authority.

Civilian authorities and the provost guard also fought a losing battle to control alcohol in Washington. Congress passed a law making it illegal to "sell, give, or administer to any soldier or volunteer in the service of the United States any spirituous liquors or intoxicating drink." Penalties included a twenty-five dollar fine or thirty days in jail.[52] Also similar to Richmond reports, regular news of citizens charged with selling alcohol to soldiers appeared in the papers.[53] In an attempt to cut soldiers off from access to alcohol, provost guards and police officers targeted restaurant owners. Raids on restaurants resulted in fines for the owners as well as arrests for soldiers.[54] In all matters of vice, authorities in both Richmond and Washington contended with soldiers who sought to enjoy what might be their final days on earth. With that kind of thought in the minds of soldiers, authorities found it increasingly difficult to bar soldiers from vices such as prostitution, alcohol, and even gambling.

The reluctance to accept the reality of their particular situation proved to be one of the biggest problems facing both cities in halting or reducing vice activities. The newspapers of Richmond refused to acknowledge food shortages early in the war. Throughout the war, the *Richmond Daily Whig* promoted "safe" jobs in munitions plants, although deadly explosions occurred from time to time. In addition, the paper only rarely hinted that destitute, rather than "morally bankrupt," women entered the sex trade. Some Northern editors likewise dismissed accusations of immorality among prominent officers and simply ignored contradictory stories.

The Richmond papers took great care in separating the moral, upstanding women from the fallen women of the community. In an article titled "The Spirit of Our Women," the editor stated that the women of Richmond showed great enthusiasm for the men, remained very moral, and volunteered their services to the war effort regularly.[55] For those women unable to volunteer, the paper advocated working in the factories making rifle cartridges. In one advertisement, the editor lauded the Thomas Factory on Bird Island claiming that the women there worked in "no fear of accident." Yet in the story above, he wrote about someone being injured at another munitions factory as a result of an "explosion of fulminating powder."[56]

The most famous instance of faulty reporting in Richmond occurred in response to what became known as the Richmond Bread Riots on April 2, 1863. The Bread Riots started because many of the poorer citizens and refugees of Richmond felt that merchants artificially raised prices to profit unfairly from wartime conditions, when inflation ultimately proved to be the cause of rising food prices. According to most reports, the initial rioters consisted of around 120 women and children breaking into stores and stealing food and other items. Contemporaries hotly debated the actual origin of the people involved. Northern newspapers characterized the rioters as starving refugees and Richmonders. Southern newspapers argued that the rioters consisted of the dregs of society. The *Memphis Daily Appeal* quoted the *Richmond Examiner*, referring to the mob as "a handful of prostitutes, professional thieves, Irish and Yankee hags, gallows birds from all lands but our own." The *Examiner* went on to argue that the "woman huckster at their head, [is the same woman] who buys veal at a toll-gate for a hundred and sells the same for two hundred & fifty in the morning market. . . ." Arguing that the mob had concealed its primary motivation of profit, the *Examiner* continued: "Under the demagogues' delusion that they might be 'poor people, starving people' and the like, an institution of charity made a distribution of rice and flour to all who would ask for it." The editor claimed the notion of charity to be ridiculous because a shortage of labor existed at the time and with acceptable wages. According the editor of the *Examiner*, "everything in human shape that is willing to work can make from two to four dollars in the day; when seamstresses refuse two dollars and a half with board, because they said board does 'not include tea and butter!'"[57]

To a degree, the editor of the *Daily Richmond Whig* agreed with the *Examiner*. The overwhelming number of refugees simply overloaded the city's resources. One year after the Bread Riots, the editor of the *Whig* stated: "there are a thousand greasy, bloated, foreign loafers, from their appearance immense consumers of both food & drink, who may be seen idling about Main Street from Spotswood corner to 20th Street, who should be sent off or driven off by some means."[58] The editor of the *Whig*, however, seemed to partially understand the economics involved. In an article titled "The cost of living," the editor printed that the cost of a cheap boarding house amounted to ninety dollars per month.[59] Even at the rate of the *Examiner*'s two dollars and a half per day, a seamstress working seven days a week would not have enough money pay for a room and the single meal that accompanied her rent.

The most outlandish of the claims printed in the *Memphis Daily Appeal* on the Bread Riot came at the end of the article. The editor alleged that the rioters from Richmond traveled to Atlanta, Petersburg, and Salisbury, starting riots there for profit.[60] For this particular editor, it proved easier to claim that a party of miscreants traveled around the

The Richmond Bread Riots. In Richmond and several other cities throughout the Confederacy, rising food prices and a lack of employment for women resulted in several acts of desperation with groups of women and children looting bakeries and other mercantiles.

Confederacy sparking riots in an elaborate scheme, rather than admitting that runaway inflation and unbearable food shortages combined to force regular people to drastic action.

The citizens of Richmond began experiencing telling shortages very early in the war. The *Richmond Whig* reported in July 1861 that "the stock of provisions is so nearly exhausted that it is unnecessary to give [price] quotations" for the markets.[61] In addition to shortages, by March 1862, Confederate money already began significantly depreciating, which caused inflation.[62] In a revealing article, the editor compared prices from 1860 to those in October 1863. According to the article, corn cost thirteen times more in 1863 than it did in 1860, and calico brought 12.5 cents per yard in 1860 but demanded six or seven dollars per yard in 1863.[63] A few days later, a report appeared stating that male clerks in Richmond earned about $1,500 a year. Ever-increasing rents along with the rising prices of food caused the editor to estimate that a man with a family would have to earn five to six thousand dollars a year to survive.[64] Given that men of the period earned significantly more than women working in "traditional" occupations, many women felt forced to do anything they could to survive. Probably feeling the pinch of inflation himself, in October 1863 the editor urged: "Gentility is no excuse for the starvation of women and children. The rich must support the poor this winter."[65] The editor's words evidently did not go unnoticed. Several days later the paper announced that the money taken in by the theater that evening would be donated to the poor.[66] Unfortunately, very little help materialized for the multitude of refugees overflowing Richmond. The terrible state of things would continue through the end of the war.

Though the poor struggled to survive in Civil War Richmond, wealthier members of society did not live through the period unscathed. Many sold valuables as a means of keeping pace with spiraling inflation. On February 24, 1863, the *Richmond Daily Whig* reported the sale of "the late President Tyler's wine stock," claiming that the collection "certainly would not be equaled in the Confederacy in these days of the blockade." With little means for luxury, most bottles sold at ten to fifteen dollars.[67] Recent arrivals routinely advertized in the newspaper offering to sell their furniture.[68] Finding themselves in unfamiliar circumstances, the wealthier portions of Richmond's population had little help to offer the poor. For those with access to some land—usually the wealthy—the *Daily Whig* began encouraging citizens to plant gardens in any available space with the hope of keeping produce prices down.[69] Although the editor did not note if his advice had been widely acted on, he continued to advocate the gardens through out the war years.[70]

The poor of Richmond could not count on the Alms House for help either. The authorities transformed the establishment into a hospital as masses of wounded soldiers returned from combat. The editor of the *Richmond Daily Whig* fired off an editorial charging that no reason existed "for longer depriving the city of the use of the Alms House for reformatory purposes. . . . Then the Council may put into operation a penal institution long needed in this city for the suppression of vice & vagrancy among juvenile & feminine delinquents."[71] Even if the city court wished to jail or attempt to reform prostitutes or other "delinquents," the city did not have a facility to house them. Finally in April 1864 the paper reported construction on a workhouse, with the Alms House back in service.[72] Though the Richmond city government likely could not have accomplished much more for the poor during the war, it is telling that the capital city of the Confederacy struggled to provide basic services for the indigent of the city. With the capital city unable to do much to help the poor during the war, other towns and cities throughout the Confederacy faced even higher odds against providing services.

Most civilians in the North experienced a drastically different war. The problems of the blockade, foraging armies, and terrible inflation did not confront the North. Like Southerners, Northerners contended with the perceived morality of their soldiers. Northern newspapers often overlooked transgressions of the most famous Union soldiers, while lampooning their Southern counterparts. On February 24, 1863, the *Daily Morning Chronicle* of Washington, D.C., reported very high morale since General Hooker became the commander of the Army of the Potomac. The paper claimed Hooker to be more efficient than previous generals with absolutely no report about allegations of debauchery.[73] Daniel Sickles, a colorful comrade of Hooker, faced no reports of any misdeeds in an article from the *Sunday Morning Chronicle* nearly a year and a half previously.[74] In the same issue, the editor reported that soldiers in some regiments busied themselves building log cabins to use as chapels and "literary rooms" while in winter quarters just outside of the capital.[75]

Although Washington, D.C., struggled to attend to the poor of the city, the issue proved less significant compared to that of Richmond. The winter of 1862–1863 found the alms house of the capital almost overflowing, but food supplies remained stable with no significant increases in price.[76] Without the masses of refugees, housing prices also remained stable in Washington. As a means of safeguarding nurses passing through the capital, the Sanitary Commission established a branch of the Washington Army Relief Station to provide temporary quarters.[77] Another group that formed during the war to aid citizens emerged as the Ladies Association for Relief of Destitute Women. The members established a group home that sheltered and fed the needy females while requesting sewing work to provide some income for the women.[78] Citizens of the capital did not face extraordinary food shortages either. Whereas Richmonders experienced incredibly expensive food staples, Washingtonians read ads in newspapers for Japanese teas and Schnapps along with patent medicines for twenty-five and fifty cents per bottle.[79] Citizens of Washington even found it within their means to purchase relatively expensive items and services such as artificial arms and legs, as well as embalming services for their relatives at a cost of twenty to fifty dollars.[80]

The comparison of the capitals, Washington, D.C., and Richmond, Virginia, depicts the difficulty and ultimate inability of either government to find an acceptable solution to issues of prostitution. In a larger sense, this secondary issue captured the overwhelming obstacles that both sides faced while trying to focus their attention on actually fighting the war. During army training, many women flocked to the staging areas of both capitals. Many, though not all, prostitutes in Richmond, initially came there as refugees and became prostitutes as a means of survival in an economic climate of surplus labor. Contrarily, many prostitutes in Washington arrived with experience as sex workers seeking to make more money than they had at their previous urban locations. Initially, the capitals took vastly different approaches in dealing with increasing numbers of prostitutes. Richmond continued a laissez faire policy of only arresting and possibly expelling prostitutes if they created major problems for the city. Washington military authorities attempted to completely suppress the sex trade for soldiers, however, arresting all military personnel found in brothels. Richmond retained its policy throughout the war, primarily because little could be done to change the situation. Although authorities in the Southern capital did not seem intent on attempting to curtail prostitution, the city had no functioning work house and very little room to incarcerate prostitutes, which would provide alternatives to the sex trade. Washington authorities had more options and ability to handle the issue, though the irrepressible tide of men seeking the services of prostitutes eventually wore down the system nevertheless. Following the initial prohibition, authorities in Washington realized the impossibility of enforcement after a Provost Marshal ruined his health by overwork and resigned. General Burnside revisited the policy and issued new orders to only arrest soldiers who were misbehaving and causing a commotion in brothels.

The editors of both cities, and many of their readers, viewed the sex trade with distaste. More moderate newspapers stereotyped the local sex workers, charging them with being citizens of extremely low class. The papers often overlooked the circumstances that placed the women in such situations, as well as the responsibility of soldiers and officers who patronized the women. Though many people and editors railed against prostitution and vice, without the money and goods provided by soldiers, the sex trade would have functioned on a much smaller scale.

Because most prostitutes found motivation in money, with those in Richmond motivated by sheer survival, authorities had a difficult time subduing the trade. The actions of the women and children in the Richmond Bread Riots reflected the economy and desperation of the people in Richmond during the war. Many Southern newspapers depicted the rioters as prostitutes and miscreants, rather than as starving civilians. Ever-worsening shortages and inflation in Richmond confronted the people of the Confederate capital, as well as the rest of the South, forcing them to adopt previously unthinkable courses of action such as entering the sex trade. Though the city attempted to help the poor through the construction of an alms house, and charity events, even the wealthy struggled during the war, and ultimately the poor usually had to fend for themselves.

Although the people of the North faced much better conditions during the war, many there also turned to prostitution as a means of providing for themselves and their families. Civilians in Washington did not face the compiled hardships of the Confederate capital, so fewer women found themselves turning to prostitution for sheer survival. Food supplies in the United States capital remained relatively stable because of a lack of foraging armies and housing costs remained unchanged as very few refugees attempted to find shelter in the capital. As a result of the secure conditions within Washington, fewer women faced the choice of starvation or becoming a prostitute.

Though the sex workers of Richmond and Washington resided in opposing capitals at war with one another, they endured the seemingly arbitrary whims of local authorities making determinations for their business. Persevering through various policy changes, occasional violence, and moralists, sex workers found an economic niche that enabled them to survive the war. Likewise, soldiers evaded military authorities when necessary, or simply found their way to vice districts when stationed near the capitals and other larger cities to obtain the company of a prostitute for a short while. Failing to understand the enduring nature of the sex trade or the economic status of most women, authorities in Washington and Richmond never effectively addressed the problems associated with prostitution.

7

Experiments with Regulation: Nashville and Memphis

The lack of a general military policy regulating the sex trade allowed several inventive officers to initiate programs to curb the spread of venereal diseases. The officers who created such programs in Memphis and Nashville boldly looked past issues of morality to focus on the detrimental effects of disease on the strength of the armies. After several attempts to control and remove prostitutes from the cities, officers adopted a policy of regulation and medical examinations to stem the spread of disease among their men.

Both Memphis and Nashville had reputations as centers of prostitution, similar to other large cities of the antebellum South. According to the 1860 census, Nashville had a population of 207 prostitutes out of a free population of 14,000.[1] Many of the women worked within a few blocks of the capitol building. This section of the city, known as Printer's Alley, sat between Union and Deaderick Streets and contained numerous brothels, gambling houses, and bars.[2] Located in a central area of the city, the small vice district generated sufficient income for sex workers, who served the traffic passing through the capital and business districts of Nashville.

As in other cities, madams typically headed the brothels of Memphis and Nashville—though references occasionally offered a male name as the manager of a brothel. The brothels of the two cities employed as many as twelve prostitutes each, with sporadic examples of families operating an establishment. These features of the brothels proved to be similar to those of Washington and Richmond. Also paralleling the two national capitals, authorities in Memphis and Nashville typically arrested only madams during brothel raids, leaving the women to continue working. Occasionally, however, authorities arrested all of the occupants of the brothel. In March 1861, police arrested five people sharing the same bed at a brothel in Memphis. This rare case of arresting prostitutes and clients suggested that, even within a brothel, social limits still existed. Authorities in Memphis seemed to saddle prostitutes with slightly heavier fines than other municipalities, ranging from ten to twenty-five dollars. Once the women paid these fines, however, they openly resumed their illegal occupations.[3]

Both cities also had trouble with the closely related vice of alcohol. The city authorities and the respective Confederate and Union commanders attempted to limit alcohol consumption. Authorities fined citizens for drunkenness and for selling alcohol on Sundays.[4] Several newspapers even attempted public shaming to limit consumption. The editor of the *Memphis Daily Appeal* wrote "Frank Fisher drank more yesterday than the law allows even to fish. He went into a saloon and, like the celebrated Oliver, he asked for more!"[5] Recognizing excessive drinking as a threat to the soldiers, the local provost marshal prohibited the "sale of ale & lager beer" a mere three days after the capture of Memphis by Union forces. The significance of the order can be seen in its prominence as General Orders No. 1.[6]

Just as with alcohol, authorities had little hope of eliminating prostitution and other vices. Methods of fining and releasing sex workers with the knowledge that they would simply return to engaging in prostitution suggest that the police may have recognized the futility in attempting to curtail prostitution. It seems more likely that a grudging tolerance of the sex trade existed in many cities. In 1863, police arrested

Lizzie Phillips, a Memphis madam, on a charge of fighting in her brothel. Phillips paid her bail of twenty-five dollars and resumed operations. The police filed no charges relating directly to prostitution for Phillips.[7] In another case, the press actually lauded the heroic actions of a local sex worker. The editor of the *Memphis Daily Appeal* wrote that a prostitute using the name Susan Striker (her real name was Julianna Johnson) challenged Charles Burton to stop abusing his wife. Burton then shot and killed Striker. The editor presented the lady as a fallen, noble woman, ending the article with "God bless her memory."[8] Departing from the usual mocking language directed at prostitutes, it seemed that society retained recognition of their status as human beings.

A significant aspect in which Nashville and Memphis differed from Washington and Richmond proved to be the plethora of newspaper advertisements for medical cures for venereal diseases. Although doctors advertized venereal disease remedies in newspapers throughout the United States and the Confederacy, the newspapers of Nashville and Memphis featured such advertisements on a daily basis. Doctor J. B. McLean's Strengthening Cordial & Blood Purifier promised to treat "diarrhea, depression, fever, bad breath, . . . falling of the womb, baroness" and other disorders.[9] Doctor John Gibbins also catered to soldiers and civilians in Memphis through advertisements in the *Memphis Avalanche*.[10] Capitalizing on American Indian folk cures, another entrepreneur touted "The Great Indian Medicine" as a cure for "mercurial & syphilitic taints."[11] With similar claims, the "Cherokee Cure" also appeared regularly in the *Memphis Daily Appeal*. "The Indian Doctor" of 100 High Street in Nashville placed advertisements in the *Nashville Daily Gazette*. The advertisement proclaimed that the doctor "has cured over 5,000 soldiers of rheumatism, chronic diarrhea, sore eyes, swelled limbs, and all diseases which camp life brings upon them without the use of mercury in any form."[12]

Advertisements for Dr. Coleman's Dispensary for Special Diseases and Dr. King's Dispensary for Private Diseases often appeared on the advertisement page of Nashville newspapers. Doctor King claimed "gonorrhea cured without nauseous medicines or interference with business" and offered to cure both gonorrhea and syphilis within a few days.[13] Doctor Coleman's pitches could usually be found in the same column with those of Doctor King. With his slogan "Nip the Evil In Its Bud," Coleman proposed "private and venereal diseases of all forms and stages speedily cured and effectually eradicated from the system. Recent cases cured in a few days." Most important for many patients, the advertisement claimed that "Dr. C's office is well arranged and persons afflicted with these diseases can have the strictest privacy."[14] As a testament to the success of their business, both Coleman and King placed advertisements in every edition of the *Nashville Daily Union*, many issues of the *Nashville Daily Gazette*, and issues of the *Nashville Dispatch*.[15] Following the occupation of Nashville, Doctor Coleman's business improved to the extent that he began including an engraved portrait of himself near the top of his advertisement in the *Nashville Daily Union*.[16]

The sheer number of advertisements directed mainly toward the treatment of venereal diseases at the least attests to the passive acceptance of prostitution and the diseases that accompanied the trade on the part of the people of Nashville and Memphis. This acceptance is very likely one of the reasons that more prostitutes journeyed to the cities after their occupation by Union troops. The grudging acceptance of the trade provided for an already established vice district and fewer issues with law enforcement. Another likely cause for the increased numbers of sex workers in Memphis and Nashville was also the primary reason that most women entered the sex trade—survival. As the "bread basket" of the Confederacy, Middle Tennessee apparently did not suffer from the same food shortages that plagued Richmond and other areas hit hard by fighting. Following the occupation by Union soldiers, the editor of the *Daily National Intelligencer* reported that food prices in Nashville appeared to be stable, and in some cases falling marginally. The price of butter fell from seventy-five cents to forty cents following the occupation.[17] The local newspaper, the *Nashville Daily Union*, reported no food shortage the following year as well, with occasional columns touting food at "reduced rates."[18]

The major concern with prostitution in Memphis and Nashville manifested once the two cities fell to Union armies in 1862. The large garrisons moving into the cities provided an economic opportunity for those women willing to engage in the sex trade. Lonely soldiers and support people such as sutlers beckoned women to the cities. Once these women arrived in large numbers, visits to sex workers became a rite of passage and a pastime for soldiers. Private Benton E. Dubbs of Ohio stated:

> there was an old saying that no man could be a soldier unless he had gone through Smokey Row [near Printer's Alley in Nashville]. . . . The street was about three fourths of a mile long and every house or shanty on both sides was a house of ill fame. Women had no thought of dress or decency. They said Smokey Row killed more soldiers than the war.[19]

According to historian James Jones,

> By June of 1863, Brigadier General R. S. Granger, in command of Nashville, was 'daily and almost hourly beset' by regimental commanders and surgeons seeking a means of ridding the city of 'the diseased prostitutes infesting it.' Action was essential 'to save the army from a fate worse . . . than to perish on the battlefield.' Prostitution itself, though physically harmless, led to venereal disease, and was equally 'annoying and destructive to the morals of the army.'[20]

As multitudes of soldiers visited the brothels of Memphis and Nashville, venereal diseases spread rapidly through the garrisons. The problem caught the military completely by surprise. With nothing in place to counter the threat of debilitating both garrisons, military commanders grasped for any solution.

At first, many military authorities simply left it up to soldiers to seek out medical attention through the regimental surgeon or from private doctors. Although soldiers had the option of seeking out the somewhat private care of a military surgeon, private doctors prided themselves on offering clandestine treatments for venereal diseases. Such a lax policy did not work for the Union garrison stationed in Nashville. A significant portion of the thirty thousand soldiers contracted various forms of venereal diseases that threatened to debilitate the army in Nashville. The military commander of Nashville had to act immediately. The initial solution evolved into a plan to simply round up groups of prostitutes and remove them from the city.

In an initial effort, Colonel George Spalding, the Provost Marshal of Nashville, rounded up a number of prostitutes, loaded them on to a train, and sent them to the commander at Louisville, Kentucky. After a relatively short trip, the women disembarked at Louisville. The much smaller garrison, and fewer potential customers, prompted the women to quickly begin making their way back to Nashville.[21] With the white prostitutes temporarily removed from the city, African American prostitutes moved into the vice district to fill the vacant economic niche. Like many other Southern sex workers, the incoming "contrabands" had no work and found it necessary to turn to prostitution as a means of fending off starvation.[22] Once the white women from Louisville returned to Nashville, the issue of prostitution in Nashville had compounded.

In July 1863, military authorities gathered a number of prostitutes from the vice district in Nashville with orders to place the women on a riverboat named the *Idahoe*, which would take them upriver.[23] The captain of the *Idahoe*, John Newcomb, protested the effort, arguing that his boat was about to begin her maiden voyage as a luxury passenger river boat and the cargo of sex workers would surely ruin the reputation of his boat. According to Newcomb:

> I protested against their putting these women on my boat, she being a new boat, only three months built, her furniture new, and a fine passenger boat. I told them it would forever ruin her reputation as a passenger boat if they were put on her (It has done so. She is now and has since been known as the floating whore house) and pointed out to them old boats that were in the service at that time which would have answered the purpose as well as mine, but no, they said I must take them. Being in the employ of the govt. and under the control of Capt. Stubbs the quartermaster, I was compelled to keep them on my boat.

Although Newcomb vehemently argued against using his boat to transport the women, Colonel Spalding won out, ordering Newcomb to accept the passengers. On July 8, 1863, Spalding had the provost guard gather a number of women and place them onto the *Idahoe*. Previous estimates claimed that anywhere from forty to fifteen hundred prostitutes from Smokey Road journeyed to the docks to take their place on the *Idahoe*.[24] Captain Newcomb, in his claim for expenses, placed the number at exactly 111 women at the beginning of the journey.[25]

Newcomb's orders stated that the *Idahoe* would steam upriver to Louisville, Kentucky, the same place that the previous group of prostitutes ended their trip a few months previously. During the trip up the Cumberland River, Newcomb faced a difficult challenge of defending his boat against "boarding parties" of men attempting to get to the women onboard the boat. "Being angered because I strove to drive them away," he explained, "both themselves and these bad women destroyed and damaged my boat and her furniture to a great extent."[26]

As the women journeyed upriver on their trip north, the local press offered its feelings on the matter. One Nashville paper claimed that, in the chaos of the apprehensions, some "respectable ladies . . . were unceremoniously marched off" and loaded onto the *Idahoe*.[27] The *Daily Press* argued that, rather than sending the women to Louisville, they should be taken to Salt Lake City, claiming that "they'd make admirable latter day saints [sic], and old Brigham would shout gloriously at their conversion."[28]

When Newcomb arrived in Louisville with his cargo of women, the garrison commander refused a second group of sex workers. Instead of allowing the women to stay in Louisville, General Boyle, the garrison commander, ordered Newcomb to keep moving north to Cincinnati and await further orders there. Before the *Idahoe* departed Kentucky, several women disembarked at Newport, Kentucky "by a writ of habeas corpus, and soon found their way back to Nashville."[29] Arriving in Cincinnati, Newcomb held the *Idahoe* on the opposite bank for thirteen days until he received orders to return to Nashville.[30] Captain Newcomb, the *Idahoe*, and the women arrived back in Nashville on August 5, 1863, having completed a journey of twenty-eight days.[31]

On the arrival of the *Idahoe* ladies, Colonel Spalding, "recognizing the failure of his attempt to revoke the women, suggested a system of licensed prostitution."[32] Spalding established a system, with the support of General Granger, to create a hospital for the examination and treatment of prostitutes with a separate hospital for soldiers. A surgeon inspected registered prostitutes on a weekly basis for a fifty-cent fee. Healthy prostitutes received a certificate of health, of which many apparently seemed quite proud. The surgeon sent infected prostitutes to a specialized hospital for their treatment alone. Furthermore, "all public women found plying their vocation without a license and health certificate" would be "incarcerated in the workhouse for . . . thirty days."[33]

Once the authorities agreed on the initial plan, the women received a deadline to get inspected and licensed by August 20, 1863.[34] As a means of enforcing the order, Spalding assigned to a sergeant the task of finding delinquent sex workers. In his report, the provost stated that the particular sergeant proved to be "one of the most vigilant and really efficient men for the position."[35] Following the primary inspections, the surgeon noted:

> It will be observed that the number reported as suffering from contagious venereal affection is surprisingly small. This may be explained; firstly; on the presumption that those knowing themselves to be diseased will avoid examination as long as possible; and secondly, from the admitted difficulty of detecting by examination the more common form of venereal disorder, (Gonorrhea) in a female desiring to conceal her condition. That cases of this kind have escaped detection, is to say the least, quite possible.[36]

The first week of the program, the surgeon examined about fifty sex workers. One of the early problems facing the program became the issue of where to place infected prostitutes. The surgeon stated in his report: "We would respectfully suggest that a hospital or dispensary for the care of those patients is imperatively needed."[37] After the establishment of the hospital, the surgeon graciously worked to treat the women as decently as possible. He ordered "wardrobes, tables, washstands, and chairs" for the rooms in the hospital.

Though the surgeon sought to make the patients comfortable and treat them with respect, some women refused to undergo examinations. In his reports the surgeon "assumed that many diseased courtesans left the city on the publication of the order rather than be subjected to hospital treatment."[38] Many women did acquiesce, however, and received inspections. By December, more than 296 sex workers underwent examinations in Nashville.[39]

Dr. R. Wallace, an observer in Nashville, made the apparently true assertion that "this is the first time and place that anything of this kind [the legalized system of prostitution] has been in our country."[40] Once the licensing system became fully established in Nashville, the city reportedly began attracting even more prostitutes. According to surgeons involved in the program, additional sex workers arrived because of perceived safety from the threat of venereal diseases.[41] Surgeon Fletcher offered an insightful assessment of the program in his notes: "After the attempt to reduce disease by the forcible expulsion of the prostitutes had, as it always has, utterly failed, the more philosophic plan of recognizing and controlling an ineradicable evil has met with undoubted success."[42] Military authorities in Memphis took note of the program and eventually moved to mirror it in the Bluff City.

Like Nashville, Memphis possessed quite a reputation as a haven for vice. Brothels and prostitutes abounded on the docks and riverfront along the Mississippi River. Some prostitutes constructed small makeshift brothels aboard flat boats on the Wolf River, an offshoot of the Mississippi.[43] According to historian Bell Wiley, the prostitutes of Memphis proved to be so numerous that they dominated public places. An Ohio captain remarked that "Memphis . . . can boast of being one of the first places of female prostitution on the continent. Virtue is scarcely known within the limits of the city."[44] Not only did sizable numbers of prostitutes work in the city, but they also held a very public role in social events. The Old Memphis Theater held balls with prostitutes playing prominent roles in the festivities.[45]

Although the women maintained a public presence in Memphis, many of the townspeople sought to force prostitutes into the shadows.

Speaking out against the balls at the Old Memphis Theater, the editor of the *Memphis Avalanche* repeatedly called for the events to be stopped.[46] The broader public also offered little compassion to those in the sex trade. During the early stages of the war, sisters Ellen and Kate Dunn attempted to leave the trade and take up "honest" work. They looked desperately for other work, but their reputation as prostitutes prevented anyone from hiring the young women. Later the Dunns faced charges of prostitution after they could not find "honest" work and reportedly left the city.[47]

Immediately after Union occupation, military authorities attempted to keep prostitutes and soldiers away from each other. On June 17, 1862, a statement appeared from Provost Marshal John H. Gould. Gould wrote: "Lewd women are prohibited from conversing with soldiers while on duty; nor will they be allowed to walk the streets after sunset. Anyone of the class indicated who shall violate this order will be conveyed across the river and will not be allowed to return to the limits of the city."[48]

Nearly a year later, the provost marshal issued another order stating that the brothels needed to be shut down, and threatened to expel prostitutes from the city and to report soldiers found with prostitutes to their commanders. Gould's orders went so far as to warn steamboat pilots that they would be fined or arrested if found transporting prostitutes into the city. The order seemed to slow the sex trade for a few months. Fifty sex workers left the city in anticipation of being forcibly removed. Wiley claimed that "by the autumn of 1863 prostitutes again were swarming the streets, and houses of ill repute were operating at full blast."[49]

Coming to the realization that the sex trade would endure, L. L. Coxe, "an inspector or agent of the US Sanitary Commission," proposed that the experiment being carried out in Nashville, be adopted in Memphis as well.[50] Coxe went to Nashville to study the system in operation. He returned to Memphis on August 26, 1864. Later that day, the commanding general of the department ordered Colonel Thomas J. Harris, the adjutant general and mayor of Memphis, to start the program as soon as possible. Five days later, a program of licensing and inspecting prostitutes began in Memphis.[51]

Licensing of Memphis sex workers started on September 30, 1864, with the women registering at an office located at 21 Union Street. The registration fee amounted to ten dollars with a charge of two dollars and fifty cents per examination. If a surgeon determined that a woman had a venereal disease during one of the weekly examinations, she reported to a city hospital on Exchange and Front Street. There she received treatment for the disease at no charge because the examination fees paid for the upkeep of the hospital. By February 1865, 134 prostitutes had registered with the program in Memphis.[52]

Going beyond the regulations of the program in Nashville, sex workers in Memphis could not engage in "street walking, soliciting, stopping, or talking with men in the streets; buggy or horseback riding through the city in daylight; wearing a showy, flash [sic] or immodest dress in public; any language or conduct in public which attracts attention; visiting the public square, the theatre, or other resorts of LADIES" [emphasis in original]. Although several of the authorities in Memphis acknowledged that venereal diseases "had not been eliminated, at least prostitution was controlled."[53] These words, and the orders that preceded them, suggest that the military and civilian authorities in Memphis, as compared to those in Nashville, seemed more concerned with quashing the raucous behavior exhibited by some of the more brash sex workers and their customers.

Both programs in Nashville and Memphis ended soon after the conclusion of the war.[54] With the Union army mustering out many soldiers, the pressing need to control prostitution near large garrisons evaporated. Reports on the programs presented a glowing success. Because germ theory did not gain widespread acceptance until nearly a decade after the end of the war, most surgeons of the period believed that available medicine could treat and cure venereal disease.[55] A medical report on the Nashville and Memphis experiments claimed that the "results were highly satisfactory." The actual result of the program proved to be the better living conditions and cleanliness of the women. The author of the report claimed: "Under these regulations a marked improvement was speedily noticed in the manner and appearance of the women. When the inspections were first enforced many were exceedingly filthy in their persons and apparel and obscene and coarse in their language, but this soon gave place to cleanliness and propriety."[56] Though their health likely improved as a result of the state of improved cleanliness and authorities attempted to quarantine infected prostitutes and soldiers, the program did little to cure cases of infection. The medical report partially overstated as it went on to claim:

> Among the difficulties to be overcome was the opposition of the public women. This has so effectively disappeared that I believe they are now earnest advocates of a system which protects their health and delivers them from quacks and charlatans. They gladly exhibit to their visitors the 'certificate' when it is asked for, a demand, I am informed, not infrequently made. The majority of the patients in the hospital are not sent from the inspection room, but consist of women who, suspecting their malady, have voluntarily come for examination and treatment.[57]

Military authorities in Nashville argued that the program became such a success that it drew prostitutes from other cities because of the "comparative protection of venereal disease which its license system afforded." As a means of proving the claim that the program operated as a success, authorities stated that most newly discovered cases of venereal diseases originated from visits to prostitutes outside of Nashville, with soldiers becoming infected prior to their arrival.[58]

Whatever the actual rates of infection during the program, or their true origins, the Union soldiers serving in the garrison at Nashville seemed to display a chivalrous relationship with the women that offered them comforting services. Following the Battle of Nashville, two local prostitutes reportedly rode out to the battlefield as a matter of curiosity, just as many people did after battles. Unfortunately, Confederate cavalrymen captured the women, believing them to be spies, and took the women to the town of Franklin to be placed under supervision in a local hotel. As the tatters of the Confederate Army of Tennessee scattered to the winds, the women found themselves under modest guard. Taking advantage of the situation, several Union soldiers, after learning of the women's situation, rode into Franklin, liberated the young damsels, and returned with them to Nashville.[59]

The major cities of the North and South had remarkably similar relationships with prostitution during the Civil War. Washington, Richmond, Nashville, and Memphis all contained sizable populations of sex workers within their cities. Furthermore, the practice that all of these cities embraced of fining and releasing prostitutes suggests that, although members of the larger population might not have approved of the sex trade, they at least tolerated the women. The advertisements for venereal disease cures in the Nashville and Memphis newspapers seem to show that the sex trade had more of a prewar presence in those cities, likely because of all of the river traffic flowing through the region. Perhaps the greater tolerance for the trade in Nashville and Memphis allowed for a more successful experiment as the program had at least passing public support.

The provost marshals in Nashville and Memphis began their programs as a means of challenging the spread of venereal diseases among the soldiers in the local garrisons. Colonel Spalding turned to the licensing program after two failed attempts to remove the prostitutes from the city. Quickly understanding that removal would not solve the problem, Spalding instituted a program of inspections and treatments for prostitutes in Nashville. Although the treatment aspect of the program did not cure the women of their diseases, the program itself may have prompted infected women to leave the city. The inspections also led to greater presentability among sex workers. Reports following the conclusion of the program claimed that, after the experiment began, the women took more pride in themselves and practiced better hygiene. It is possible, however, that these changes came about in an effort to appear healthier for the medical inspector. Whatever the motive for such actions, the overall health of the women likely improved as a result of their efforts at cleanliness.

Noting the reported success of the Nashville program, military authorities in Memphis duplicated the program in their city. The Memphis experiment had a greater number of rules pertaining to the behavior of the prostitutes, suggesting that, in addition to venereal disease, the raucous behavior by the prostitutes demanded a significant amount of attention from the authorities.

Both programs ended at the conclusion of the war because soldiers mustered out of the army and many sex workers found other employment. As prostitutes worked in cities and towns prior to the war, the occupation continued to be a viable source of income after the war, although to a much less extent than during the war years. Army medical staff reported the programs to be successful in curing and preventing venereal diseases. Unfortunately, insufficient medical understanding of the diseases prevented their actual cure at that time, allowing their carriers to go on to spread the diseases further after the war. Civil War experiments with regulation of the sex trade foreshadowed later efforts that proved increasingly successful from a health aspect following the addition of cures for several venereal diseases in the mid-twentieth century.

Conclusion

The social landscape of the 1830s and 1840s fostered a legacy of conflicting ideas about sexuality that would color much of the debate about prostitution during the US Civil War. The rapid growth of cities, changes brought about by the Industrial Revolution, and the accompanying expansion of vice conflicted with previously held social norms. Young men moved to the cities in great numbers and discovered a tremendous opportunity to engage in vice under the protection of anonymity. At the same time, many young single women found themselves in urban areas, unable to fully support themselves. Some of these women used occasional acts of prostitution to supplement their income. The sex trade often paid more than the limited number of traditional occupations available to women.

In response to concerns about the moral direction of the country, moralists sought to reverse what they saw as a nudge down the "slippery slope" of hedonism. The Magdalen Society, one of the most famous of these groups, organized in New York City in an effort to rescue prostitutes from what society members believed to be a life of degradation. The society found itself at conflict with members of Tammany Hall after both organizations misled New Yorkers concerning the numbers of prostitutes in the city. Magdalen Society members overestimated the numbers in an attempt to obtain increased funds for their programs, whereas Tammany Hall understated the numbers to assuage fears of widespread vice. Several other groups in the North sprang up and aligned themselves on both sides of the morality issue.

Southerners largely maintained consistent ideas regarding sexuality and gender roles. As a whole, Southerners made efforts to keep Southern women within their traditional gender roles. Larger Southern cities and towns departed from this model somewhat. In this environment, Southern women became teachers, business owners, government clerks, as well as finding other means of employment on a limited scale. The rigid adherence to such roles, however, left many women at a disadvantage during the war. This disadvantage led many women into the occupation of sex work.

Men in both regions of the country held conflicting views on the sex trade. Many men of the younger generation acted on more permissive attitudes toward sexuality and prostitution. Some subscribed to the images of caution and morality espoused by groups such as the YMCA, and later, the Christian Commission. Beliefs of older officers similarly diverged. Select officers attempted to regulate the morality of camp life, whereas others allowed permissive environments to flourish in their camps. Generals such as Daniel Sickles and Joseph Hooker became famous for their hedonistic camp life, just as reformers such as the YMCA and the Christian Commission attempted to quell what they perceived as immoral activity in camp.

Primarily, women engaged in sex work during the Civil War for survival. Many women lost a central source of income during the war: their husbands, fathers, and brothers. Social norms frequently left women with few options for supporting themselves. Northern women had a few more opportunities for employment than did Southern women, although women of both regions faced economic hardship. Although both Northern and Southern women sometimes found work as clerks or teachers, most continued working on a farm, or expanded traditional female work, such as washing clothes or sewing. Unfortunately, with so many other women offering the same services, wages for such work dropped dramatically. With runaway inflation compounding the situation in the South, many Confederate citizens faced uncertain economic circumstances. Although aid societies formed during the first year of the war, and even expanded their services in later years, they could not bridge the vast economic gap facing many Southerners. The impoverished and struggling female refugees had to provide for themselves, with many turning to prostitution. Local governments in the Union and Confederacy attempted to curtail the sex trade. Such efforts typically did not have much impact because the governments faced the much larger issues of the war. Eventually, most municipalities only tried to control the sex trade by arresting prostitutes if they caused trouble. Rural women who sold sex did not remain in the business long enough to attract much attention from authorities because their customers remained attached to passing armies and left quickly.

Many women traded sex for money, but those who traded for foodstuffs captured the core of the issue of prostitution existing as a means of survival. After the war ended and soldiers mustered out to return home, so did most Civil War prostitutes. The lack of steady customers and the absence of scavenging armies simply removed the customers and the motivations for entering the sex trade. The public no longer had to fear or endure the presence of roaming armies and could migrate back to their original homes to resume their previous lives. Most prostitutes did not continue in the trade, which lends credence to the argument that most prostitutes sold sex as a means of survival and not because of base immorality.

Civil War soldiers engaged in vice for a number of reasons. Some soldiers embraced their newfound freedom of being away from the social confines of their hometowns. The absence of oversight by the larger community, as well as peer pressure from comrades, encouraged many young soldiers to explore all that the world had to offer. Other soldiers endeavored to live their lives to the fullest, believing that they would not survive the war. Visiting prostitutes carried the risk of infections with venereal diseases. Soldiers met a wide variety of stances by commanders in regard to the sex trade. Larger aspects of the war often demanded officers' attentions, which allowed many soldiers to freely seek out women. Whatever their reasons for visiting prostitutes, Civil War soldiers sought out such women, risking personal disease, and collectively threatening to prolong the war through the infection of thousands of men. The soldiers who sought to secure their self-imposed sense of morality often joined larger groups of young men for mutual support, such as the US Christian Commission or the YMCA. These soldiers, like their antebellum counterparts, attempted to safeguard the morality of their fellow members and spread their message to other soldiers.

Confederate and Union officer corps attracted to their ranks a wide variety of men with divergent personalities and beliefs. Commanders independently acted in what they believed to be the best interests of their men with regard to issues of morality and a great many other aspects of military life. As a result, soldiers experienced a staggering variety of policies addressing prostitution. Most commanders probably ignored the issue as long as soldiers fulfilled their military obligations and did not cause problems. Commanders at Nashville and Memphis, though, recognized the inevitably of soldiers seeking out prostitutes and attempted to make the sex trade as safe as possible by regulating health conditions. Other general officers objected to the trade and attempted to stop visits to prostitutes. George McClellan opposed the issue, citing discipline in the army, and possibly with added bias from having personally contracted a venereal disease. Many objections also originated from religious backgrounds. Many officers had strong religious convictions, and encouraged the same religious adherence and morality among their men. Only men under the direct supervision of such religious officers had to maintain the appearance of morality. The regiments of enlisted men relied on the anonymity of sheer numbers to help conceal their questionable behaviors. Finally, a relative few general officers appeared to endorse the sex trade. Generals Daniel Sickles, Judson Kilpatrick, and Joseph Hooker had reputations in the general public for consorting with prostitutes. Some generals made no attempt to hide their numerous trysts. Policies of opposing, endorsing, or being apathetic toward the sex trade affected many thousands of enlisted men and junior grade officers. Taken as a whole, the widely divergent policies on the sex trade espoused by general officers reflected the social conflicts over sexuality and vice that existed among members of the public.

Nearly 200,000 soldiers contracted gonorrhea and syphilis, taking the diseases to their wives and girlfriends following the war. Once infected, soldiers looked to a variety of ineffective treatments. Injections and vapor treatments of mercury and applications of silver nitrate did nothing to cure the infections. The army did not provide accessible medical care for all enlisted soldiers. African American regiments received a much lower level of care than did white soldiers. Almost every disease faced by white soldiers was present to a much higher degree among African American soldiers, with the exception of venereal diseases. African American soldiers faced public scrutiny, less availability of prostitutes, and undesirable locales, which, ironically, reduced their exposure to venereal diseases. Infection rates proved to be even lower among both African American and white sailors. Sailors serving on the blockade did not see land for months at a time, and their rare shore leaves usually did not offer to access to women. Riverine forces, however, typically patrolled near cities with large riverfront populations and sizeable numbers of prostitutes.

Just as some officers attempted to bar soldiers from consorting with prostitutes, reform groups, such as the Christian Commission and the Sanitary Commission, also worked to safeguard the spiritual lives of soldiers. Although both organizations looked to improving the lives of soldiers, the Christian Commission mainly attended to the spiritual needs of the ranks. Likewise, the US Sanitary Commission formed to aid the medical corps through dietary supplements, education, and the provision of literature to soldiers. Unfortunately, these goals often had to be placed to the side to address more important issues facing the men. One of those serious issues proved to be scurvy. The lack of fresh fruits and vegetables threatened to kill some men. Most regiments likely had some issue with venereal diseases; however, the problems that affected the largest number of men required the most attention from aid groups. Thus, venereal diseases and general vice often went unaddressed among the ever-growing issues for Civil War commanders and reformers.

Commanders and reformers searched for solutions to the issue of prostitution and so did the capitals of the United States and the Confederacy. The comparison of the capitals demonstrated that, although both municipalities had troubles addressing prostitution, the cities went about the attempt in remarkably similar ways. During the training of soldiers, in both capitals women arrived by the hundreds. Many women came to Richmond as refugees and became prostitutes in an effort to survive in the midst of surplus labor. By contrast, many prostitutes in

Washington previously had been sex workers in other places and sought to make more money than they had at their previous locations. Initially, the cities tried different methods of dealing with increasing numbers of prostitutes. Richmond authorities only arrested and expelled prostitutes if they created major problems for the city. City officials retained a lax policy throughout the war, simply because they could do little else. Washington military authorities initially tried to completely suppress the sex trade among the military, arresting all soldiers discovered in brothels. Eventually the unending numbers of men seeking the services of prostitutes caused authorities to pursue a different course. In 1863 Generals Ambrose Burnside and Hooker drastically changed the policy by issuing new orders to arrest only those soldiers causing problems in brothels, while concentrating the sex trade in one area.

Newspaper editors in both cities, as well as many of their readers, disliked the sex trade. Some editors quietly remarked on their displeasure over the prostitute issue, whereas others cried foul to the heavens over the situation. Unfortunately, these papers often disregarded the desperate situations facing many of these women and ignored the mutual responsibility of soldiers and officers who patronized the women. Though many people and editors argued for abolishing the sex trade, without the money and foodstuffs provided by soldiers to prostitutes they certainly would not have been as prominent a feature of urban areas.

Because most prostitutes worked to support themselves, at times for sheer survival, authorities faced an almost impossible task in eliminating or fully controlling the sex trade. The actions of the women and children of the Richmond Bread Riots reflected the complete desperation of many people in Richmond during the war. Many Southern newspapers depicted the rioters as prostitutes and miscreants, often claiming that the mob did not reside in Richmond, but was made up of outsiders. Yet ever-tightening shortages and inflation in Richmond simply left people of that city with few options. As a result, the rioters felt themselves forced to adopt previously unthinkable courses of action, such as rioting or entering the sex trade. Though the city attempted to help the poor through the construction of an alms house, holding charity events, and even opening up food stores meant for the armies, such tactics only partially alleviated the suffering. Even the wealthy struggled to survive during the war, and, ultimately, the poor largely had to fend for themselves.

Though they had more opportunities for employment, rarely faced armies campaigning through their communities, and did not endure such inflated food prices, some women in the North engaged in the sex trade. Some of the women had previously worked as poorly paid or part-time prostitutes and saw an economic opportunity in catering to soldiers. Other women in the North, facing hardships related to absent or deceased husbands during the war also entered the sex trade as a means of survival.

Sex workers of Richmond and Washington had remarkably similar experiences in relation to local society and the governments. Enduring policy changes, occasional violence, and reformers, sex workers found an economic niche that allowed them to eke out a living. Never really grasping the basic motivations behind the sex trade, authorities in Washington and Richmond did not effectively come to terms with its causes or the impact the industry had on the armies.

The cities of Washington, Richmond, Nashville, and Memphis all contained great numbers of prostitutes. Sex workers lived in a state of limbo in all of these cities. Subject to fines, but quickly released to engage in their trade to pay those fines, many of the women existed outside the law, yet subject to it. The recurrent advertisements touting venereal disease cures in the Nashville and Memphis newspapers depict a strong prewar presence of the sex trade in those cities, likely related to the river traffic flowing through the region.

Once the war began, venereal diseases presented a problem for military authorities. The provost marshals in Nashville and Memphis instituted regulatory programs in hopes of quelling the spread of venereal diseases among the soldiers in their garrisons. Colonel George Spalding started the licensing program after at least two attempts to remove most of the prostitutes from the city. Eventually grasping the idea that removal would not solve the problem, Spalding enacted a program of inspections and treatments for prostitutes in Nashville. Although the military prescribed medical care did not cure the soldiers or women of their diseases, the program itself may have encouraged sex workers infected with diseases to flee the city. The program also may have prompted the women to take greater care with their appearance and adopt better hygiene. Rather than being instigated by increased pride of being in the program, it is possible that improvements in hygiene stemmed from an effort by the prostitutes to convince the medical inspector of overall health. Based on the reported success of the Nashville program, military authorities in Memphis mirrored the licensing experiment. Memphis authorities instituted a greater number of rules pertaining to the behavior of the prostitutes in an effort to control the spread of infection and to maintain social standards.

Both programs ended as troops left their posts following the war. The lack of customers forced some sex workers to find other employment. The Union medical reports claimed that the programs operated as successful efforts to cure and prevent venereal diseases. Unfortunately, the available treatments simply masked symptoms rather than actually cured venereal diseases, although inspections of prostitutes by military doctors seemed to improve overall health and living conditions among the sex workers. The experiments in regulation foreshadowed similar efforts later in urban areas of the United States.

The impact of prostitution and venereal diseases probably did not have the potential to change the course of the war. The impact of the sex trade during the 1860s did have the potential to influence the duration of the war to a slight degree. Some officers in both armies attempted to limit the impact that prostitution had on the physical health of their men, fearing epidemics of venereal diseases could ravage the armies if unchecked. It is possible that such widespread diseases could have withered the ranks. Because more Union soldiers served in stationary garrisons with more visits by the paymaster than their Confederate counterparts, more Union soldiers had both the opportunity and financial ability to patronize prostitutes and possibly contract a venereal disease. Yet the advantage of Union manpower countered the overall impact of that problem. Because the field armies of both sides remained on the move or in rural camps they faced less exposure to prostitutes and fewer chances to contract venereal disease.

The effects of the sex trade during the Civil War persisted for years following their initial manifestations. Civil War prostitution seems to have produced at least three impacts on life in the postwar period. As Catherine Clinton suggested, the increase in prostitution during the war fostered some tenacious negative views of women in public life. Prior to the war years, many young men sought out virtuous women for marriage. The idea that such women remained plentiful seemed to vanish. As an unnamed comrade of Captain Charles Hayden remarked, many men may have given up on finding a virginal bride and only hoped to find a woman who did not have a venereal disease. Although many people held a diminished image of women's morality following the war, that image did not remain unchecked. Female participation in the US Christian Commission, the US Sanitary Commission, nursing, and other charitable activities served to counter the image of female immorality. Nursing proved to be one of the most effective occupations for changing female imagery. As more and more women entered the profession during the war, nursing transitioned from an occupation staffed by men and women of lower status, to one dominated by socially respectable women.

The second lasting effect of the sex trade proved to be the near-epidemic infections of venereal diseases. Venereal diseases, rather than most other ailments, probably had the greatest impact on the postwar health of those infected. More than 109,000 Union soldiers contracted gonorrhea during the war with another 73,382 infected with syphilis.[1] Although gonorrhea manifested itself quickly, syphilis often lay dormant with serious symptoms and death years later. Not only did those initially infected during the war suffer, but infection rates also increased through the transmission of the disease to spouses and other intimates.

The third impact prostitution had on later society emerged as scattered experiments in public policy regarding the regulation of the sex trade. Although wartime efforts at regulation of the sex trade yielded only limited results, they may have been influential in stimulating later attempts at urban regulation of prostitution. For example, the city of St.

Louis, Missouri, initiated a program in 1870 that closely mirrored the Nashville and Memphis experiments. Rather than fighting a constant battle to quash prostitution within the city, the local government chose to regulate the sex trade by charging brothels and their occupants a licensing fee as well as requiring regular medical inspections. The program ended in 1874 amid legal entanglements and a moralist outcry to end the "social evil ordinance."[2] Similar debates over attempts at regulation would follow in a few other late nineteenth-century United States cities.

An Evening with Venus: Prostitution during the American Civil War reflects an attempt to capture the realities and remove some of the romanticized notions of the sex trade. The sex trade during the Civil War created far-reaching implications on an individual as well as social level. Prostitution during the Civil War expanded to involve thousands of men and women, which stirred extensive debate, but probably did not have a major impact on the conflict itself. The effects of wartime prostitution on the status of women, the increased ravages of venereal diseases, and attempts at regulating the sex trade did play a significant role in US society during and after the war.

Notes

Introduction

1. Frederick Henry Dyer, ed., *The Civil War CD-ROM: The War of the Rebellion, A Compilation of the Union and Confederate Armies* (Carmel: Guild Press of Indiana, 1996), Series I, Volume XLIX, 1108.
2. Dyer, ed., *The Civil War CD-ROM.*
3. No substantiating information has been located. Several conversations with National Park Service staff at the Andrew Johnson Home failed to produce a clear consensus on the issue.
4. Burke Davis, *The Civil War: Strange and Fascinating Facts* (New York: Fairfax Press, 1982), 158.
5. Davis, *The Civil War,* 162.
6. Thomas P. Lowry, *The Story the Soldiers Wouldn't Tell: Sex in the Civil War* (Mechanicsburg, PA: Stackpole Books, 1994).
7. Catherine Clinton, *Public Women and the Confederacy* (Milwaukee: Marquette University Press, 1999).
8. Christine Stansell, *City of Women: Sex and Class in New York: 1789–1860* (Champaign: University of Illinois Press, 1987), 186.
9. Stansell, *City of Women,* 163.
10. Timothy Gilfoyle, *City of Eros: New York City, Prostitution, and the Commercialization of Sex, 1790–1920* (New York: W. W. Norton & Co., 1994).
11. Victoria E. Bynum, *Unruly Women: The Politics of Social and Sexual Control in the Old South* (Chapel Hill: University of North Carolina Press, 1992).
12. Anne Butler, *Daughters of Joy, Sisters of Misery: Prostitutes in the American West, 1865–90* (Champaign: University of Illinois Press, 1987).
13. Ruth Rosen, *The Lost Sisterhood: Prostitution in America, 1900–1918* (Baltimore, MD: Johns Hopkins University Press, 1982).

1

1. Catherine Clinton, "'Public Women' and Sexual Politics during the American Civil War," in *Battle Scars: Gender and Sexuality in the American Civil War*, edited by Catherine Clinton and Nina Silber (New York: Oxford University Press, 2006), 61.
2. Amy Gilman Srebnick, *The Mysterious Death of Mary Rogers: Sex and Culture in Nineteenth-Century New York* (New York: Oxford University Press, 1995), 8.
3. Helen Lefkowitz Horowitz, *Rereading Sex: Battles over Sexual Knowledge and Suppression in Nineteenth-Century America* (New York: Alfred A. Knopf, Inc., 2002), 301.

4. Patricia Cline Cohen, *The Murder of Helen Jewett: The Life and Death of a Prostitute in Nineteenth Century New York* (New York: Alfred A. Knopf, Inc., 1998), 10.

5. Horowitz, *Rereading Sex*, 301.

6. Horowitz, *Rereading Sex*, 301.

7. Karen Halttunen, *Confidence Men and Painted Women: A Study of Middle-class Culture in America, 1830–1870* (New Haven, CT: Yale University Press, 1982), 1-2.

8. Cohen, *The Murder of Helen Jewett*, 201.

9. Halttunen, *Confidence Men and Painted Women*, 5.

10. Cohen, *The Murder of Helen Jewett*, 67.

11. Horowitz, *Rereading Sex*, 146.

12. Horowitz, *Rereading Sex*, 125.

13. John Todd, *The Young Man: Hints Addressed to the Young Men of the United States* (Northhampton, PA: J. H. Butler, 1845), 122.

14. Susan E. Cayleff, *Wash and Be Healed: The Water-Cure Movement and Women's Health* (Philadelphia: Temple University Press, 1987), 51.

15. Horowitz, *Rereading Sex,* 125.

16. Srebnick, *The Mysterious Death of Mary Rogers*, 53.

17. Cohen, *The Murder of Helen Jewett*, 65.

18. *Richmond Daily Whig* (Richmond, Virginia), 5 August 1864; *Memphis Daily Appeal* (Memphis, Tennessee), 2 April 1863.

19. Horowitz, *Rereading Sex*, 145.

20. Cohen, *The Murder of Helen Jewett*, 68–69.

21. Horowitz, *Rereading Sex*, 145.

22. Horowitz, *Rereading Sex*, 171.

23. Butler, *Daughters of Joy, Sisters of Misery*, 60.

24. Elizabeth A. Topping, *What's a Poor Girl to Do?: Prostitution in Mid-Nineteenth-Century America* (Gettysburg, PA: Thomas Publications, 2001), 13.

25. Stansell, *City of Women*, 186–187.

26. Cohen, *The Murder of Helen Jewett*, 23.

27. Cohen, *The Murder of Helen Jewett*, 19.

28. Cohen, *The Murder of Helen Jewett*, 24.

29. Cohen, *The Murder of Helen Jewett*, 29.

30. Cohen, *The Murder of Helen Jewett*, 20.

31. Horowitz, *Rereading Sex*, 171.

32. Cohen, *The Murder of Helen Jewett*, 63.

33. Horowitz, *Rereading Sex*, 151.

34. Horowitz, *Rereading Sex*, 146.

35. Horowitz, *Rereading Sex*, 145.

36. Horowitz, *Rereading Sex*, 148.

37. Horowitz, *Rereading Sex*, 147.
38. Horowitz, *Rereading Sex*, 148.
39. Horowitz, *Rereading Sex*, 45.
40. Horowitz, *Rereading Sex*, 148.
41. Horowitz, *Rereading Sex*, 49. This argument is similar to the claims made in late 2006 against the vaccine for human papillomavirus—a virus that is associated with cervical cancer in women. Socially conservative groups claimed that the vaccine would encourage promiscuity. Like free thinkers of the 1830s, some doctors and other progressive thinkers argued to the contrary. According to Doctor Christine Peterson, "The presence of seat belts in cars doesn't cause people to drive less safely. The presence of a vaccine in a person's body doesn't cause them to engage in risk-taking behavior they would not otherwise engage in." Although conservative groups in 2006 did not state that the vaccine promoted the "temptations of the devil," their core argument was the same. See: "Lifesaving Politics," *Ms. Magazine*, Spring 2007, pp 12–13.
42. Horowitz, *Rereading Sex*, 54.
43. Horowitz, *Rereading Sex*, 57.
44. Horowitz, *Rereading Sex*, 60.
45. Horowitz, *Rereading Sex*, 56.
46. Horowitz, *Rereading Sex*, 62.
47. Horowitz, *Rereading Sex*, 300.
48. Horowitz, *Rereading Sex*, 304.
49. Horowitz, *Rereading Sex*, 330.
50. Horowitz, *Rereading Sex*, 305.
51. Gerald Linderman, *Embattled Courage: The Experience of Combat in the American Civil War* (New York: The Free Press, 1987), 8.
52. Bynum, *Unruly Women*, 21.
53. Bynum, *Unruly Women*, 55.
54. Bynum, *Unruly Women*, 55.
55. Bynum, *Unruly Women*, 56.
56. Bynum, *Unruly Women*, 45.
57. Madaline Selima Edwards, *Madaline: Love and Survival in Antebellum New Orleans*, edited by Dell Upton (Athens: University of Georgia Press, 1996), 9.
58. Edwards, *Madaline*, 9.
59. Edwards, *Madaline*, 166.
60. Edwards, *Madaline*, 79, 174, and 189.
61. Bynum, *Unruly Women*, 93.
62. Bynum, *Unruly Women*, 93.
63. Bynum, *Unruly Women*, 97.

2

1. Horowitz, *Rereading Sex*, 394.
2. During the summer of 2007, the Justice Ministry in Britain even considered removing the term *prostitute* from the legal code because of the stigma it carries. "Britain to delete term 'prostitute' from law books." Accessed August 14, 2005, at http://today.reuters.com.
3. Bynum, *Unruly Women*, 21.
4. Nancy Woloch, *Women and the American Experience*, 4th ed. (Boston: McGraw Hill, 2006), 145.
5. Springer, *The Preachers Tale,* 21
6. William J. Cooper, Jr. and Thomas E. Terrill, *The American South: A History*, 3rd ed. (Boston: McGraw Hill, 2002), 267.
7. Ernest B. Furguson, *Ashes of Glory: Richmond at War* (New York: Alfred A. Knopf, 1996), 75.
8. *Memphis Daily Appeal* (Memphis), 5 April 1861.
9. Bynum, *Unruly Women*, 55.
10. Bynum, *Unruly Women*, 21.
11. Bynum, *Unruly Women*, 25, 52.
12. Bynum, *Unruly Women*, 56.
13. Suzanne Lebsock, *The Free Women of Petersburg: Status and Culture in a Southern Town, 1784–1860* (New York: W. W. Norton & Company, 1984), 190.
14. Lebsock, *The Free Women of Petersburg* 112, 116.
15. Woloch, *Women and the American Experience*, 144.
16. Woloch, *Women and the American Experience*, 143.
17. *Memphis Daily Appeal* (Memphis, Tennessee), 28 August 1861; *Daily National Intelligencer* (Washington, D.C.), 3 March 1864.
18. Woloch, *Women and the American Experience*, 144.
19. George C. Rable, *Civil Wars: Women and the Crisis of Southern Nationalism* (Urbana: University of Illinois, 1989), 112, 129, 133.
20. *Richmond Daily Whig* (Richmond, Virginia), 22 July 1861, and 21 April 1863. See also, *Richmond Examiner* (Richmond, Virginia), 14 March 1863. *Richmond Dispatch* (Richmond, Virginia), 4 July 1861, 28 January, 1862 and 6 August 1862. *Richmond Enquirer* (Richmond, Virginia), 14 March 1863.
21. Drew Gilpin Faust, *Mothers of Invention: Women of the Slaveholding South in the American Civil War* (Chapel Hill: University of North Carolina Press, 1996), 82, 100.
22. Woloch, *Women and the American Experience*, 218, 219.
23. Rable, *Civil Wars*, 112; Edwards, *Madaline*, 9, 166; and *Daily Richmond Whig*, 15 October 1863.
24. See Maraget Leech, *Reveille in Washington: 1860–1865* (New York: Harper & Row Publishers, 1941; Repr., New York: Carrol & Graf Publishers, Inc.

1991), 128. Thomas H. O. O'Connor, *Civil War Boston: Home Front & Battlefield* (Boston: Northeastern University Press, 1997), 204.

25. *Daily Morning Chronicle* (Washington, D.C.), 24 February 1863.

26. Springer, *The Preacher's Tale*, 18.

27. *Richmond Whig*, 20 July 1861; *Daily Richmond Whig*, 4 July 1863, 9 October 1863, and 13 April 1864.

28. *Richmond Daily Whig* (Richmond, Virginia), 15 April 1864.

29. *Richmond Daily Whig*, 30 April 1864 and 10 August 1864.

30. *Richmond Daily Whig*, 31 January 1862.

31. *Richmond Daily Whig*, 20 July 1861.

32. *Richmond Daily Whig*, 12 July 1861.

33. *Richmond Daily Whig*, 4 July 1863.

34. Butler, *Daughters of Joy, Sisters of Misery*, 15.

35. Susan Barber, "Depraved and Abandoned Women: Prostitution in Richmond, Virginia, across the Civil War," in *Neither Lady nor Slave: Working Women of the Old South*, edited by Susanna Delfino and Michele Gillespie (Chapel Hill: University of North Carolina Press, 2002), 163.

36. *Nashville Daily Union* (Nashville, Tennessee), 8 July 1863, and *Nashville Dispatch* (Nashville, Tennessee), 26 and 28 July 1863.

37. Barber, "Depraved and Abandoned Women," 159.

38. August Scherneckau, *Marching with the First Nebraska: A Civil War Diary*, edited by James E. Potter and Edith Robbins (Norman: University of Oklahoma Press, 2007), 128–131.

39. *Richmond Dispatch*, 13 May 1862.

40. Bell I. Wiley, *The Life of Billy Yank* (Indianapolis: Bobbs-Merrill Company, 1951), 257.

41. Lowry, *The Story the Soldiers Wouldn't Tell*, 65.

42. *Richmond Whig* (Richmond, Virginia), 17 July 1861.

43. *Daily Morning Chronicle* (Washington, D.C.), 23 February 1863.

44. *Richmond Whig*, 12 July 1861.

45. *Richmond Whig*, 12 July 1861.

46. *Richmond Whig*, 17 July 1861.

47. *Richmond Whig*, 20 July 1861.

48. *Daily Richmond Whig*, 30 July 1864. For other similar instances see, *Daily Richmond Whig*, 3 September 1861 and 23 July 1864, and *Richmond Whig*, 12 July 1861.

49. *Memphis Daily Appeal* (Memphis, Tennessee), 5 April 1861.

50. Springer, *The Preacher's Tale*, 14.

51. Bell Irvin Wiley, *Confederate Women: Beyond the Petticoat* (Westport, CT: Greenwood Publishing, 1975. Repr., New York: Barnes & Noble Press, 1994), 162.

52. Wiley, *Confederate Women*, 162.

53. Wiley, *Confederate Women*, 162.

54. Wiley, *Confederate Women*, 163.

55. Jennifer Lynn Gross, "And for the Widow & Orphan? Confederate Widows, Poverty, & Public Assistance," in *Inside the Confederate Nation: Essays in Honor of Emory M. Thomas*, edited by Lesley J. Gordon and John C. Inscoe (Baton Rouge: Louisiana State University Press, 2005), 215, 216.

56. Gross, "And for the Widow & Orphan?" 162.

57. *Memphis Daily Appeal*, 28 August 1861; *Daily Richmond Whig*, 13 April 1864.

58. Clinton, "'Public Women'," 63.

59. Personal letter from _____ to Jane Trail. February 16, 1866. Collection of Elizabeth Topping.

60. Barnes, Joseph K. *The Medical and Surgical History of the War of the Rebellion, 1861–65. Prepared in accordance with the acts of Congress, under the direction of Surgeon General, Joseph K. Barnes, United States Army.* 6 Volumes. (Washington, D.C.: Government Printing Office, 1870–1888. Repr., Wilmington, NC: Broadfoot Publishing Company, 1991), I: 891–892.

61. Wiley, *The Life of Billy Yank*, 257. Barnes, ed., *The Medical And Surgical History of the Civil War*, I: 894. Military authorities recorded 456 licensed prostitutes in Nashville at the height of the licensing program. Although some sources give an often repeated number of two thousand, the total number of prostitutes likely did not reach such a high number. It is highly likely that this number was somewhat higher because some sex workers operated covertly and evaded the provost marshals.

62. Butler, *Daughters of Joy, Sisters of Misery*, 41. See also *Daily Morning Chronicle*, 23 February, 1863; *Daily Richmond Whig*, 5 August 1864; and *Memphis Daily Appeal*, 2 April 1863.

63. *Richmond Dispatch*, 13 May 1862, and *Nashville Daily Union*, 29 May 1863, and 8 July 1863.

64. Pierce Letter, 7 July 1863 (Tullahoma, Tennessee). Motlow College Civil War Research Center. Accessed October 30, 2007, at www.cwrc.org.

65. Clinton, "'Public Women'," 70.

66. *Nashville Dispatch*, 22 December 1864.

67. Woloch, *Women and the American Experience*, 221.

68. Faust, *Mothers of Invention*, 88, 89.

3

1. Howard Malcolm Hannah, "Confederate Action in Franklin County, Tennessee," *Franklin County Historical Review* 23 (1992): 3–4.

2. *Home Journal* (Winchester, Tennessee), 10 November, 1859.

3. *Home Journal*, 20 January 1860, 20 October 1859, and 8 December 1859, and *Winchester Appeal* (Winchester, Tennessee), 16 February 1856.

4. Michael D. Foreman, "The Secession of Franklin County," *Franklin County Historical Review: The War of 1861–1865, A Franklin County Perspective* 28 (Winchester, Tennessee: Franklin County Historical Society, 1998), 10.

5. *Daily Richmond Whig* (Richmond, Virginia), 9 May 1862.

6. *Daily Richmond Whig*, 9 May 1862.

7. *Richmond Whig* (Richmond, Virginia), 23 July 1861. This is the same newspaper as the *Daily Richmond Whig;* sometime in late 1861 or early 1862 the paper simply became a daily and changed the name.

8. *Memphis Daily Appeal* (Memphis, Tennessee), 3 April 1861.

9. *Daily National Intelligencer* (Washington D.C.), 29 August 1861. For other examples of newspaper propaganda regarding morality see *Richmond Whig*, 23 July 1861, and *Richmond Daily Whig*, 3 July 1861.

10. Wiley, *The Life of Billy Yank*, 261.

11. James M. McPherson, *For Cause and Comrades: Why Men Fought in the Civil War* (Cambridge, Massachusetts: Oxford University Press, 1998), 62.

12. McPherson, *For Cause and Comrades*, 64.

13. James I. Robertson, Jr., *Soldiers Blue and Gray* (Columbia: University of South Carolina Press, 1998), 95.

14. Sam R. Watkins, *Co. Aytch: A Memoir of the Civil War* (New York: Touchstone, 2003), 99.

15. Wiley, *Life of Billy Yank*, 258–259.

16. John Bennitt, M.D., *"I Hope to Do My Country Service": The Civil War Letters of John Bennitt, M. D., Surgeon, 19th Michigan Infantry*, edited by Robert Beasecker (Detroit, Michigan: Wayne State University Press, 2005), 329.

17. Scherceckau, *Marching with the First Nebraska*, 160, 161.

18. Lawrence Murphy, "The Enemy among Us: Venereal Disease among Union Soldiers in the Far West," *Civil War History* 31 (1985), 263.

19. Reid Mitchell, *Civil War Soldiers* (New York: Penguin Classics, 1997), 122.

20. Mitchell, *Civil War Soldiers*, 122.

21. Charles Tubbs, *Mr. Tubbs' Civil War*, edited by Nat Brandt (Syracuse, NY: Syracuse University Press, 1996), 52.

22. Wiley, *Life of Billy Yank*, 258.

23. Clinton, "'Public Women'," 63.

24. Lawrence, "The Enemy among Us," 263.

25. *Sexual Transmitted Diseases Guide: Online Version*. Accessed October 21, 2007 at http://std-gov.org/stds/gonorrhea.htm.

26. Freeman J. Bumstead, M.D., "Venereal Diseases," in *Military Medical and Surgical Essays Prepared for the United States Sanitary Commission*, edited by William A. Hammond, M.D. (Philadelphia: J. B. Lippincott & Co., 1864), 531–552.

27. Lawrence, "The Enemy among Us," 258.

28. Barnes, *Medical and Surgical History of the Civil War*, VI: 893, 894.

29. *Richmond Daily Whig*, 12 January 1863.

30. *Memphis Daily Appeal*, 29 March 1861.

31. *Memphis Daily Appeal*, 28 March 1861.

32. Loose advertisement by D. E. Young of Philadelphia, Pennsylvania. From the private collection of Elizabeth Topping.

33. Jefferson B. Fancher, M.D., *Medical, Matrimonial, and Scientific Expositor; Giving the Most Important Information Upon Every Subject Relating to Man and Woman* (New York: Author, 1867).

34. Walter H. Herbert, *Fighting Joe Hooker* (Lincoln: University of Nebraska Press, 1999). Thomas Keneally, *American Scoundrel: The Life of the Notorious Civil War General Dan Sickles* (New York: Nan A. Talese, 2002). Samuel J. Martin, *Kill-Cavalry: The Life of Union General Hugh Judson Kilpatrick* (Mechanicsburg, PA: Stackpole Books, 2000). W. A. Swanberg, *Sickles the Incredible* (New York: Charles Scribner's Sons, 1956). Ulysses S. Grant, *The Personal Memoirs of Ulysses S. Grant* (Old Sybrook, CT: Konecky & Konecky, 1992).

35. *Daily National Intelligencer* (Washington, D.C.), 12 October 1861. Bell I. Wiley, *The Life of Johnny Reb* (Indianapolis: Bobbs-Merrill Company, 1943), 53. A further exploration of officers' efforts to either limit access to prostitutes or widespread infections with venereal diseases will be discussed in the chapter on officers and the chapter on Nashville and Memphis.

36. Major Harvey Brown to Lieutenant Colonel E. D. Townsend, 13 May 1861, *Official Records of the War of the Rebellion* (Washington, D.C.: Government Printing Office, 1880–1901), Series I, volume I, 407–408. Hereafter cited as *O.R.* Report by Brigadier General J. Bankhead Magruder, C.S. Army, 9 August 1861, *The War of the Rebellion*, Series I, IV: 572.

37. J. Franklin Dyer, *The Journal of a Civil War Surgeon*, edited by Michael B. Chesson (Lincoln; University of Nebraska Press, 2003), 51.

38. Dyer, *The Journal of a Civil War Surgeon*, 24.

39. Bennitt, "I Hope to Do My Country Service," 292, 302.

40. Pierce Letter, 7 July, 1863 (Tullahoma, Tennessee). Motlow College Civil War Research Center. Accessed October 30, 2007, at www.cwrc.org.

41. Francis Springer, Reverend, *The Preacher's Tale: The Civil War Journal of Rev. Francis Springer, Chaplain, U.S. Army of the Frontier*, edited by William Furry (Fayetteville: University of Arkansas Press, 2001), 14.

42. Springer, *The Preacher's Tale*, 18.

43. *Daily National Intelligencer*, 3 March 1864.

44. Court-martial of Captain Jerome B. Taft, 86th New York Volunteers. *Records of the Office of the Judge Advocate General* RG 153, II 704. National Archives, Washington, D.C.

45. Court-martial of Joseph Meekins. *Quartermaster Records Consolidated Correspondences File*, 1794–1915. RG 92, entry 225. National Archives, Washington, D.C.

46. Court-martial of Private H. C. Steel, 3rd Illinois Cavalry Volunteers. *Records of the Office of the Judge Advocate General* RG 153, LL 25 47. National Archives, Washington, D.C.

47. Scherceckau, *Marching with the First Nebraska*, 139.

48. Scherceckau, *Marching with the First Nebraska*, 132.

49. Charles J. Stille, *History of the United States Sanitary Commission, Being the General Report of Its Work during the War of the Rebellion* (Philadelphia; J. B. Lippincott & Co., 1866), 25.

50. Stille, *History of the United States Sanitary Commission*, 24.

51. Stille, *History of the United States Sanitary Commission*, 21, 22.

52. Joel Molyneax, *Quill of the Wild Goose: Civil War Letters and Diaries of Private Joel Molyneax, 141st P. V.*, edited by Kermit Molyneax Bird (Shuppensburg, PA: Burd Street Press, 1996), 176.

53. Wiley, *The Life of Billy Yank*, 261.

54. Joseph T. Glatthaar, "The Costliness of Discrimination: Medical Care for Black Troops in the Civil War," in *Inside the Confederate Nation: Essays in Honor of Emory M. Thomas*, edited by Lesley J. Gordon and John C. Inscoe (Baton Rouge: Louisiana State University Press, 2005), 252.

55. Glatthaar, "The Costliness of Discrimination," 253.

56. Glatthaar, "The Costliness of Discrimination," 257.

57. Glatthaar, "The Costliness of Discrimination," 260.

58. Steven J. Ramold, *Slaves, Sailors, Citizens: African Americans in the Union Navy* (DeKalb: Northern Illinois University Press, 2002), 105.

59. Ramold, *Slaves, Sailors, Citizens*, 101.

60. Ramold, *Slaves, Sailors, Citizens*, 106.

61. Unsigned letter to unnamed official, August 1864, in *Freedom's Soldiers: The Black Military Experience in the Civil War*, edited by Ira Berlin, Joseph P. Reidy, and Leslie S. Rowland (New York: Cambridge University Press, 1998), 127.

62. Thomas Sipple to President Abraham Lincoln, August 1864, in *Free at Last: A Documentary History of Slavery, Freedom, and the Civil War*, edited by Ira Berlin et al. (New York: New Press, 1992), 475.

63. Soldiers from the 33rd USCT to General Daniel Sickles, January 1866, in *Freedom's Soldiers*, 171.

64. Barnes, *The Medical And Surgical History of the Civil War*, VI: 891.

65. Barnes, *The Medical And Surgical History of the Civil War*, VI: 891.

66. Report by Commander George Henry Preeble, US Navy, commanding USS *St. Louis*, 23 July 1864, *Official Records of the Union and Confederate Navies in the War of the Rebellion*. (Washington, D.C.:

Government Printing Office, 1896), Series I, II: 123. Hereafter cited as *Navy O.R.*

67. Michael J. Bennett, *Union Jacks: Yankee Sailors in the Civil War* (Chapel Hill: University of North Carolina Press, 2003), 61.

68. Bennett, *Union Jacks*, 119.

69. Spoford, Tileson, & Co. to Secretary of the Navy, Gideon Welles, 5 September 1861, *Navy O.R.* Series I, I: 85.

70. Spoford, Tileson, & Co. to Secretary of the Navy, Gideon Welles, 5 September 1861, 69.

71. Spoford, Tileson, & Co. to Secretary of the Navy, Gideon Welles, 5 September 1861, 80–81; Report by Lieutenant Commander Lowery, US Navy, US supply steamer *Union*, 19 May 1863, *Navy O.R.* Series I, XXVII: 499.

72. Bennett, *Union Jacks*, 80, 85.

73. Darla Brock, "Memphis's Nymphs Du Pave: 'The Most Abandoned Women in the World," *West Tennessee Historical Society's Papers* 50 (Memphis: West Tennessee Historical Society, 1996), 60.

74. *Memphis Daily Appeal* (Memphis, Tennessee), 27 August 1861.

75. Wiley, *The Life of Billy Yank*, 260.

76. A more elaborate description of these groups will be found in Chapter 5.

77. Bumstead, M.D., "Venereal Diseases," 531–552.

4

1. Ivan Musicant, *Divided Waters: The Naval History of the Civil War* (New York: Harper Collins Publishers, 1995), 3.

2. David S. Sparks, ed., *Inside Lincoln's Army: The Diary of Marsena Rudolph Patrick, Provost Marshal General, Army of the Potomac* (New York: A. S. Barnes and Company, 1964), 70.

3. Sparks, *Inside Lincoln's Army*, 72.

4. Sparks, *Inside Lincoln's Army*, 96–97.

5. Sparks, *Inside Lincoln's Army*, 256.

6. Murphy, "The Enemy among Us," 263.

7. *Daily Richmond Whig*, 15 May 1862.

8. Joseph H. Parks, *General Leonidas Polk C. S. A.: The Fighting Bishop* (Baton Rouge: Louisiana State University Press, 1962), 96.

9. Parks, *General Leonidas Polk C. S. A.*, 306.

10. General Robert McAllister, *The Civil War Letters of General Robert McAllister*, edited by James I. Robertson, Jr. (New Brunswick, NJ: Rutgers University Press, 1965), 6.

11. McAllister, *The Civil War Letters of General Robert McAllister*, 13.

12. McAllister, *The Civil War Letters of General Robert McAllister*, 14.

13. *Daily National Intelligencer* (Washington, D.C.), 12 October 1861.

14. John C. Waugh, *The Class of 1846: From West Point to Appomattox: Stonewall Jackson, George McClellan and their Brothers* (New York: Ballantine Publishing Group, 1994), 167.

15. Waugh, *The Class of 1846*, 166.

16. Waugh, *The Class of 1846*, 166.

17. Stephen W. Sears, *George B. McClellan: The Young Napoleon* (New York: Da Capo Press, 1999; Repr., Boston: Ticknor and Fields, 1988), 61.

18. Wiley, *The Life of Johnny Reb*, 53.

19. Wiley, *The Life of Johnny Reb*, 53.

20. Clinton, "'Public Women'," 63.

21. Peter Cozzens and Robert I. Girardi, eds., *The Military Memoirs of General John Pope* (Chapel Hill: University of North Carolina Press, 1998), 25, 27.

22. *Daily Richmond Whig*, 9 May 1862.

23. James Boyd Jones, Jr. "A Tale of Two Cities: The Hidden Battle against Venereal Disease in Civil War Nashville and Memphis." *Civil War History* 31 (1985): 270.

24. Jones, "A Tale of Two Cities," 271.

25. Barnes, M.D., *The Medical And Surgical History of the Civil War*, VI: 894.

26. Brock, "Memphis's Nymphs Du Pave," 64

27. Brock, "Memphis's Nymphs Du Pave," 65.

28. James B. Jones, Jr. "Municipal Vice: The Management of Prostitution in Tennessee's Urban Experience. Part I." *Tennessee Historical Quarterly* 50, no. 1 (1991): 35.

29. Edward Longacre, *The Commanders of Chancellorsville: The Gentleman vs. The Rogue* (Nashville: Rutledge Hill Press, 2005), 104.

30. Burke Davis, *The Civil War: Strange & Fascinating Facts* (Austin: Holt, Rinehart, and Winston, Inc, 1996; Repr., New York: Wings Books, 1960), 158.

31. Charles Francis Adams, *Charles Francis Adams: An Autobiography* (Boston: Houghton Mifflin Company, 1916), 161.

32. George Templeton Strong, *The Diary of George Templeton Strong: Post-War Years, 1865–1875* (New York: The Macmillan Company, 1952), 422.

33. Swanberg, *Sickles the Incredible*, 92.

34. *New York Times*, 12 April 1859.

35. Swanberg, *Sickles the Incredible*, 54.

36. *New York Times*, 12 April 1859.

37. *Richmond Daily Whig*, 3 July 1861. The *Daily Richmond Whig* and the *Richmond Daily Whig* were apparently the same newspaper organization. For several months during 1861, the paper adopted the name: *Richmond Daily Whig*. In 1862, the paper changed their name yet again to the *Daily Richmond Whig*.

38. Julia Lorrilard Butterfield, ed., *A Biographical Memorial of General Daniel Butterfield: Including Many Addresses and Military Writings* (New York:

Grafton Press, 1904), 160; Swanberg, *Sickles the Incredible*, 175. Although Swanberg claimed that only the Princess kissed Lincoln, he cited Butterfield as the source of his statement. She claimed that several of the women kissed Lincoln.

39. Butterfield, *A Biographical Memorial of General Daniel Butterfield*, 161.
40. Butterfield, *A Biographical Memorial of General Daniel Butterfield*, 161–162.
41. James H. Kidd, *One of Custer's Wolverines: The Civil War Letters of Brevet Brigadier General James H. Kidd, 6th Michigan Cavalry*, edited by Eric J. Wittenberg (Kent, Ohio: Kent State University Press, 2000), 49.
42. Martin, *Kill-Cavalry*, 62.
43. Martin, *Kill-Cavalry*, 128.
44. Martin, *Kill-Cavalry*, 128.
45. Martin, *Kill-Cavalry*, 131.
46. Martin, *Kill-Cavalry*, 131.
47. Davis, *Civil War: Strange & Fascinating Facts*, 162.
48. Davis, *Civil War: Strange & Fascinating Facts*, 162, 163.
49. Elizabeth Bacon Custer, *The Civil War Memories of Elizabeth Bacon Custer: Reconstructed from Her Notes and Diaries*, edited by Arlene Reynolds (Austin: University of Texas Press, 1994), 49.
50. Custer, *The Civil War Memories of Elizabeth Bacon Custer*, 52.
51. W. W. Davis, "Cavalry Service under General Wheeler," *Confederate Veteran* August 1903, 353; W. W. Davis, "Kilpatrick's Spotted Horse," *Confederate Veteran*, February 1906, 62; Martin, *Kill-Cavalry*, 199.
52. Major General Benjamin Butler, *Butler's Book: Autobiography and Personal Reminisces of Major-General Benjamin F. Butler* (Boston: A. M. Thayer & Co., 1892), 415.
53. Butler, *Butler's Book*, 418.
54. Faust, *Mothers of Invention*, 209.
55. Butler, *Butler's Book*, 418.
56. Butler, *Butler's Book*, 417.
57. Major General Benjamin Butler: General Orders No. 28. *O.R.* Series I, XV: 426.
58. James Parton, *General Butler in New Orleans: History of the Administration of the Department of the Gulf in the year 1862: With an Account of the Capture of New Orleans and a Sketch of the Previous Career of the General, Civil and Military* (New York: Mason Brothers, 1864), 327.
59. Butler, *Butler's Book*, 418.
60. Clinton, "'Public Women'," 66.
61. *Picayune* (New Orleans), 15 May 1862.
62. Parton, *General Butler in New Orleans*, 328.
63. Parton, *General Butler in New Orleans*, 328.

64. *Picayune*, 17 May 1862.

65. *Picayune*, 17–31 May 1862.

66. Parton, *General Butler in New Orleans*, 328.

67. *Daily Richmond Whig*, 7 June 1862.

68. A Proclamation by President Jefferson Davis, 23 December 1862. *O.R.* Series 1, XV: 906.

69. A Proclamation by President Jefferson Davis, 23 December 1862.

70. Faust, *Mothers of Invention*, 210.

71. *Daily National Intelligencer* (Washington, D.C.), 30 May 1862.

72. *Daily National Intelligencer* (Washington, D.C.), 31 May 1862.

73. Clinton, "'Public Women'," 65.

5

1. Frank R. Freemon, *Gangrene and Glory: Medical Care During the American Civil War* (Madison, NJ: Fairleigh Dickinson University Press, 2000), 23.

2. Freemon, *Gangrene and Glory*, 19.

3. Freemon, *Gangrene and Glory*, 23.

4. Freemon, *Gangrene and Glory*, 24.

5. *Daily National Intelligencer* (Washington, D.C.), 24 March 1862, and 1 November 1861.

6. Cayleff, *Wash and Be Healed*, 55.

7. *Daily National Intelligencer*, 29 August 1861 and 26 March 1862.

8. *Daily National Intelligencer*, 2 April 1862.

9. *The Memphis Daily Appeal*, 28 March 1861.

10. Lawrence, "The Enemy among Us," 264.

11. Freemon, *Gangrene and Glory*, 26.

12. Bumstead, "Venereal Diseases," 545–546.

13. Centers for Disease Control and Prevention, Syphilis Fact Sheet, accessed July 30, 2008, at http://www.cdc.gov/std/Syphilis/STDFact-Syphilis.htm.

14. Bumstead, "Venereal Diseases," 542.

15. Bumstead, "Venereal Diseases," 547.

16. Bumstead, "Venereal Diseases," 550.

17. Bumstead, "Venereal Diseases," 549.

18. Bumstead, "Venereal Diseases," 551.

19. Barnes, *The Medical And Surgical History of the Civil War*, VI: 891.

20. Report by Surgeon J. G. Brandt, New Orleans, Louisiana, 1 January 1863, in Barnes, *The Medical And Surgical History of the Civil War*, VI: 892.

21. Report by Surgeon Ezra Read, Baltimore, Maryland, 1 September 1861, in Barnes, *The Medical And Surgical History of the Civil War*, VI: 892.

22. Agency for Toxic Substances and Disease Registry, ToxFAQs for Mercury, accessed July 30, 2008, athttp://www.atsdr.cdc.gov/tfacts46 .html#bookmark04.

23. Brandt in Barnes, *The Medical And Surgical History of the Civil War*, VI: 892.
24. MayoClinic.com, Orchitis, accessed July 31, 2008, at http://www .mayoclinic.com/health/orchitis/DS00602.
25. Bumstead, "Venereal Diseases," 536.
26. Bumstead, "Venereal Diseases," 532.
27. Horace Herndon Cunningham, *Doctors in Gray: The Confederate Medical Service* (Baton Rouge: Louisiana State University Press, 1958), 211.
28. Report by Surgeon A. F. Peck, Los Lunas, New Mexico, September 1862, in Barnes, *Medical and Surgical History*, VI: 892; Assistant Surgeon P. W. Randall, Fort Bragg, California, 1 June 1863, in Barnes, *Medical and Surgical History*, VI: 892. Note: Randall filed his report from Fort Bragg, California, a post that existed from 1857 until 1864.
29. Bumstead, "Venereal Diseases," 534.
30. Barbara Chubak, personal communication, 27 April 2007.
31. Steven E. Woodworth, *While God Is Marching On: The Religious World of Civil War Soldiers* (Lawrence: University Press of Kansas, 2001), 161, 166.
32. Woodworth, *While God Is Marching On*, 186, 188.
33. *Daily National Intelligencer*, 2 April 1861.
34. *Daily National Intelligencer*, 9 September 1861.
35. *Daily National Intelligencer*, 14 September 1861.
36. *Daily National Intelligencer*, 16 September, 1861.
37. Horowitz, *Rereading Sex*, 308.
38. Horowitz, *Rereading Sex*, 306.
39. Horowitz, *Rereading Sex*, 308.
40. *Daily National Intelligencer*, 23 August 1861.
41. *Daily National Intelligencer*, 25 October 1861.
42. Horowitz, *Rereading Sex*, 309.
43. Horowitz, *Rereading Sex*, 305.
44. John Bennitt, "I hope to Do My Country Service," 282.
45. *Richmond Whig*, 16 July 1861.
46. *Daily Richmond Whig*, 15 May, 1862.
47. *Daily Morning Chronicle* (Washington, D.C.), 24 February 1863.
48. *Daily National Intelligencer* (Washington, D.C.), 29 March 1862, and 2 June 1862.
49. Robert H. Bremmer, *The Public Good: Philanthropy and Welfare in the Civil War Era* (New York: Alfred A. Knopf, 1980), 79.
50. Bremmer, *The Public Good*, 47.
51. Bremmer, *The Public Good*, 45.
52. Stille, *History of the United States Sanitary Commission*, 25.
53. Stille, *History of the United States Sanitary Commission*, 22, 26.
54. Stille, *History of the United States Sanitary Commission*, 21–22.

55. William Quentin Maxwell, *Lincoln's Fifth Wheel: The Political History of the United States Sanitary Commission* (New York: Longmans, Green, & Co., 1956), 295.

56. Maxwell, *Lincoln's Fifth Wheel*, 23.

57. Maxwell, *Lincoln's Fifth Wheel*, 36, 50, 54, 46.

58. Strong, *The Diary of George Templeton Strong*, 244–246.

59. Dyer, *The Journal of a Civil War Surgeon*, 178.

60. Bennitt, "I hope to Do My Country Service," 302.

61. *Nashville Dispatch*, 8, 10, 26, 28 July 1863.

62. *Nashville Daily Union*, 8 July 1863.

63. Report by Surgeon Robert Fletcher, Nashville, Tennessee, 15 August 1864, in Barnes, *Medical and Surgical History*, VI: 894.

64. Report by Surgeon Robert Fletcher, Nashville, Tennessee, 15 August 1864, 893–894.

65. Report by Surgeon Robert Fletcher, Nashville, Tennessee, 15 August 1864, 894–895.

66. "Disneyland East," *Time Magazine,* May 6, 1966, accessed August 10, 2008, at http://www.time.com/time/magazine/article/0,9171,901833,00.html.

6

1. Bennett, *Union Jacks*, 80.

2. *Richmond Daily Whig* (Richmond, Virginia), 5 July 1861.

3. *Richmond Daily Whig* (Richmond, Virginia), 6 November 1861.

4. Ernest B. Furgurson, *Ashes of Glory: Richmond at War* (New York: Alfred A. Knopf, 1996), 55.

5. Furgurson, *Ashes of Glory*, 44.

6. *Richmond Daily Whig*, 9 December 1861.

7. *Richmond Daily Whig*, 14 March 1862.

8. Kenneth Radley, *Rebel Watchdog: The Confederate States Army Provost Guard* (Baton Rouge: Louisiana State University Press, 1989), 60.

9. *Richmond Daily Whig*, 16 December 1861, and 14 March 1862; and *Richmond Dispatch* (Richmond, Virginia), 13 May 1862.

10. Furgurson, *Ashes of Glory*, 62.

11. *Richmond Daily Whig*, 11 December 1861.

12. *Richmond Daily Whig*, 16 December 1861.

13. *Richmond Daily Whig*, 14 March 1862 and 16 February 1863.

14. *Richmond Dispatch*, 13 May 1862.

15. Furgurson, *Ashes of Glory*, 100.

16. Clinton, "'Public Women'," 62.

17. *Daily Mississippian* (Jackson), 8 April 1863.

18. *Richmond Daily Whig*, 30 April 1864.

19. Ernest B. Furgurson, *Freedom Rising: Washington in the Civil War* (New York: Alfred A. Knopf, 2004), 207.

20. Wiley, *The Life of Billy Yank*, 257.

21. *Daily Morning Chronicle* (Washington, D.C.), 23 February 1863.

22. *Daily Morning Chronicle* (Washington, D.C.), 23 February 1863.

23. *Daily Morning Chronicle* (Washington, D.C.), 30 January, 1863.

24. Leech, *Reveille in Washington*, 263.

25. Leech, *Reveille in Washington*, 261.

26. Furgurson, *Freedom Rising*, 207.

27. *Daily National Intelligencer* (Washington, D.C.), 2 August 1861.

28. *Daily National Intelligencer* (Washington, D.C.), 12 October 1861.

29. *Daily National Intelligencer* (Washington, D.C.), 27 December 1861.

30. Reports on Washington, D.C. 27 July 1861–9 November 1862. *Official Records of the War of the Rebellion* (Washington, D.C.: Government Printing Office, 1880–1901), Series I, V: 29.

31. Washington, D.C. orders. Records of the Office of the Judge Advocate General RG 393, Volume I, 5441. National Archives, Washington, D.C.

32. Leech, *Reveille in Washington*, 261.

33. Headquarters Department of Washington—Office of Provost Marshal General, April 1, 1865, *OR*, Series I, XLVI: 1097.

34. Davis, *Strange & Fascinating Facts*, 158.

35. *Richmond Daily Whig*, 2 September 1861.

36. Furgurson, *Ashes of Glory*, 56.

37. Furgurson, *Ashes of Glory*, 61.

38. *Richmond Whig*, 16 July 1861; *Richmond Daily Whig*, 12 January 1863.

39. *Daily National Intelligencer*, 30 September 1861.

40. Leech, *Reveille in Washington*, 262.

41. *Daily National Intelligencer*, 30 September 1861.

42. *Daily National Intelligencer*, 23 October 1861.

43. *Daily National Intelligencer*, 29 July 1861. Court-martial of Captain Jerome B. Taft, RG 153, II 704. Court-martial of Joseph Meekins. RG 92, entry 225. Court-martial of Private H. C. Steel, RG 153, LL 25 47.

44. Leech, *Reveille in Washington*, 260.

45. Leech, *Reveille in Washington*, 261–262.

46. *Richmond Daily Whig*, 14 March 1862.

47. *Richmond Daily Whig*, 7 December 1861.

48. *Richmond Whig* (Richmond, Virginia), 17 July 1861; *Richmond Daily Whig*, 26 January 1863, 15 April 1864, and 16 April 1864.

49. Furgurson, *Ashes of Glory*, 60.

50. *Richmond Daily Whig*, 9 May 1862.

51. *Richmond Daily Whig*, April 1864.

52. *Daily National Intelligencer,* 29 July 1861.

53. *Sunday Morning Chronicle* (Washington, D.C.), 8 September 1861; *Daily National Intelligencer*, 4 September 1861, and 8 October 1861.

54. *Daily National Intelligencer*, 10 September 1861.

55. *Richmond Daily Whig*, 5 June 1862.

56. *Richmond Whig*, 22 July 1861.

57. *Richmond Examiner*, quoted in the *Memphis Daily Appeal* (Jackson, Mississippi), 13 April 1863.

58. *Richmond Daily Whig*, 13 April 1864.

59. *Richmond Daily Whig*, 9 October 1863.

60. *Richmond Examiner*, 13 April 1863.

61. *Richmond Whig*, 19 July 1861.

62. *Richmond Daily Whig*, 14 March 1862.

63. *Richmond Daily Whig*, 9 October 1863.

64. *Richmond Daily Whig*, 9 October 1863.

65. *Richmond Daily Whig*, 9 October 1863.

66. *Richmond Daily Whig*, 14 October 1863.

67. *Richmond Daily Whig*, 24 February 1863.

68. *Richmond Daily Whig*, 31 January 1862 and 4 July 1863.

69. *Richmond Daily Whig*, 4 March 1863.

70. *Richmond Daily Whig*, 15 April 1864.

71. *Richmond Daily Whig*, 12 February 1863.

72. *Richmond Daily Whig*, 20 April 1864.

73. *Daily Morning Chronicle*, 24 February 1863.

74. *Sunday Morning Chronicle*, 8 December 1861.

75. *Sunday Morning Chronicle*, 8 December 1861.

76. *Daily Morning Chronicle*, 30 January 1863; *Daily National Intelligencer*, 11 March 1863.

77. *Daily National Intelligencer*, 11 March 1863.

78. *Daily National Intelligencer*, 3 March 1864.

79. *Daily National Intelligencer*, 6 August 1863 and 11 August 1863.

80. *Daily National Intelligencer*, 1 November 1861 and 2 April 1862.

7

1. Clinton, "'Public Women'," 63.

2. *Nashville Daily Union* (Nashville, Tennessee), 15 February 1863. This area of the city remains a popular night time attraction with bars and strip clubs in the twenty-first century.

3. Brock, "Memphis's Nymphs Du Pave," 59, 60.

4. *Memphis Daily Appeal* (Memphis, Tennessee), 4 April 1861; *Nashville Daily Union*, 15 February 1863.

5. *Memphis Daily Appeal*, 6 April 1861.

6. *The Bulletin* (Memphis, Tennessee), 9 July 1862.

7. *Memphis Daily Appeal*, 5 April 1863.

8. *Memphis Daily Appeal*, 5 April 1861.

9. *Memphis Daily Appeal*, 27 August 1861.

10. *Memphis Avalanche* (Memphis, Tennessee), 5 March 1861.

11. *Memphis Daily Appeal*, 29 August 1861.

12. *Nashville Daily Gazette* (Nashville, Tennessee), 15 March 1864.

13. *Nashville Daily Union*, 15 February 1863.

14. *Nashville Daily Union*, 15 February 1863.

15. *Nashville Daily Gazette*, 13 March 1864; *Nashville Dispatch* (Nashville, Tennessee), 17 March 1865.

16. *Nashville Daily Union*, 29 May 1863.

17. *Daily National Intelligencer* (Washington, D.C.), 31 March 1862.

18. *Nashville Daily Union*, 11 June 1863.

19. Jones, "A Tale of Two Cities," 271.

20. Jones, "A Tale of Two Cities," 271.

21. Lowry, *The Story the Soldiers Wouldn't Tell*, 78. Ephraim A. Wilson, *Memoirs of the War by Captain Ephraim A. Wilson, of Co. "G," 10th Illinois Veteran Volunteer Infantry* (Cleveland: W. M. Bayne Printing Co., 1893), 151. Lowry cited Captain Ephraim Wilson's memoirs for the number of "1,500" prostitutes. This number seems to be an accidental overestimate by Wilson based on the later removal of 111 prostitutes by riverboat. Such a huge number does not seem plausible.

22. Jones, "A Tale of Two Cities," 272.

23. Barnes, *The Medical And Surgical History of the Civil War*, VI: 893.

24. Jones, "A Tale of Two Cities," 272.

25. Captain John M. Newcomb claim for expenses and damages to the *Idahoe*. Record Group 29, State Historian Box 23, Folder 19 "War Between the States, 1955–1958." Tennessee State Library and Archives.

26. Captain John M. Newcomb claim for expenses and damages to the *Idahoe*.

27. Jones, "A Tale of Two Cities," 272.

28. Jones, "A Tale of Two Cities," 273.

29. *Medical and Surgical History*, VI: 893. These writs likely came from a civilian court because they are identified as coming from anonymous men who served the captain these papers.

30. Captain John M. Newcomb claim for expenses and damages. The source for the order remains unclear.

31. *Nashville Dispatch* (Nashville, Tennessee), 5 August 1863.

32. *Medical and Surgical History*, VI: 893.

33. Jones, "A Tale of Two Cities," 273.

34. *Medical and Surgical History*, VI,: 893.

35. Office of Provost Marshal, Medical Department. RG 94, File A388, entry 621. National Archives, Washington, D.C.

36. *Nashville Dispatch* (Nashville, Tennessee), 22 August 1863.
37. *Nashville Dispatch*, 26 August 1863.
38. *Nashville Dispatch,*, 9 September 1863. Barnes, *Medical and Surgical History*, VI: 893.
39. Office of Provost Marshal, Medical Department, 21 December 1863.
40. Jones, "A Tale of Two Cities," 273.
41. Jones, "Municipal Vice," 33.
42. Barnes, *Medical and Surgical History*, VI: 894.
43. Brock, "Memphis's Nymphs Du Pave," 60.
44. Wiley, *The Life of Billy Yank*, 260.
45. Brock, "Memphis's Nymphs Du Pave," 60.
46. Brock, "Memphis's Nymphs Du Pave," 60.
47. Brock, "Memphis's Nymphs Du Pave," 63.
48. Brock, "Memphis's Nymphs Du Pave," 64.
49. Wiley, *The Life of Billy Yank*, 260; Brock, "Memphis's Nymphs Du Pave," 65.
50. Barnes, *Medical and Surgical History*, VI: 894.
51. Barnes, *Medical and Surgical History*, VI: 895.
52. Brock, "Memphis's Nymphs Du Pave," 66.
53. Jones, "Municipal Vice," 35.
54. Jones, "A Tale of Two Cities," 276.
55. Jones, "Municipal Vice," 35.
56. Barnes, *Medical and Surgical History*, VI: 894.
57. Barnes, *Medical and Surgical History*, VI: 894.
58. Barnes, *Medical and Surgical History*, VI: 894.
59. *Nashville Dispatch*, 22 December 1864.

Conclusion

1. Murphy, "The Enemy among Us," 258.
2. James Wunsch, "The Social Evil Ordinance," *American Heritage Magazine* 33 no. 2 (1982), accessed February 25, 2009 at http://www.americanheritage.com/articles/magazine/ah/1982/2/1982_2_50_print.shtml.

Bibliography

Primary Sources

Letter to Jane Trail. February, 16, 1866. Collection of Elizabeth Topping.

Young, D. E. Loose advertisement from Philadelphia, Pennsylvania. Collection of Elizabeth Topping.

Archival Materials

Office of the Provost Marshal, Medical Department. RG94. National Archives, Washington, D.C.

Pierce Letter. Motlow College Civil War Research Center. Tullahoma, Tennessee.

Quartermaster Records Consolidated Correspondences File, 1794–1915. RG 92. National Archives, Washington, D.C.

Records of the Office of the Judge Advocate General. RG 153. National Archives, Washington, D.C.

Records of the Office of the Judge Advocate General. RG 393. National Archives, Washington, D.C.

State Historian Box 23, Folder 19 "War Between the States, 1955–1958." RG 29. Tennessee State Library and Archives.

Union Provost Marshal, File of Individual Citizens. Microfilm Collection. National Archives.

Union Provost Marshal, File of Two or More Citizens. Microfilm Collection. National Archives.

Union Provost Marshal's File of Two- or More-Named Papers Relating to Citizens. RG 109. National Archives, Washington, D.C.

War Department. Collection of Confederate Records. National Archives, Washington, D.C.

Newspapers

Congressional Globe (Washington, D.C.), 1860–1865.

Constitutional Union (Washington, D.C.), 1860–1865.

Daily Chronicle (Washington, D.C.), 1860–1865.

Daily Mississippian (Jackson), 1863.

Daily Morning Chronicle (Washington, D.C.), 1860–1865.

Daily National Intelligencer (Washington, D.C.), 1860–1865.

Daily Picayune (New Orleans, Louisiana). 1860–1865.

Daily Richmond Whig (Richmond, Virginia), 1862–1865.

Evening Star (Washington, D.C.), 1860–1865.

Home Journal (Winchester, Tennessee), 1859–1860.

Memphis Appeal (Memphis, Tennessee), 1863–1865.

Memphis Avalanche (Memphis, Tennessee), 1861.

Memphis Daily Appeal (Memphis, Tennessee), 1861–1863.

Nashville Daily Gazette (Nashville, Tennessee), 1864.

Nashville Daily Union (Nashville, Tennessee), 1862–1865.

Nashville Dispatch (Nashville, Tennessee), 1862–1865.

National Republican (Washington, D.C.), 1860–1865.

New York Times (New York, New York), 1859.

Picayune (New Orleans, Louisiana), 1861–1865.

Richmond Daily Whig (Richmond, Virginia), 1861–1862.

Richmond Dispatch (Richmond, Virginia), 1861–1862.

Richmond Enquirer (Richmond, Virginia), 1863.

Richmond Examiner (Richmond, Virginia), 1863.

Richmond Whig (Richmond, Virginia), 1861–1862.

Southern Illustrated News (Richmond, Virginia), 1860–1865.

Sunday Morning Chronicle (Washington, D.C.), 1860–1865.

The Bulletin (Memphis, Tennessee), 1862.

Winchester Appeal (Winchester, Tennessee), 1856.

Government Documents

Barnes, Joseph K. *The Medical and Surgical History of the War of the Rebellion, 1861–65. Prepared in accordance with the acts of Congress, under the direction of Surgeon General, Joseph K. Barnes, United States Army.* 6 Volumes. Washington, D.C.: Government Printing Office, 1870–1888. Reprint, Wilmington, NC: Broadfoot Publishing Company, 1991.

Beers, Henry Putney. *Guide to the Archives of the Government of the Confederate States of America.* Washington, D.C., 1968.

Bumstead, M. D., Freeman J. "Venereal Diseases." In *Military Medical and Surgical Essays Prepared for the United States Sanitary Commission,* 531–552. Edited by William A. Hammond, M. D. Philadelphia: J. B. Lippincott & Co., 1864.

Confederate States War Department. *Regulations for the Army of the Confederate States, 1863.* Richmond, 1863.

Dyer, Frederick Henry, ed. *The Civil War CD-ROM: The War of the Rebellion, A Compilation of the Union and Confederate Armies.* Carmel: Guild Press of Indiana, 1996.

Journal of the Congress of the Confederate States of America, 1861–1865. 7 Volumes. Washington, D.C., 1904–1905.

Official Records of the Union and Confederate Navies in the War of the Rebellion. Washington, D.C.: Government Printing Office, 1896.

Official Records of the War of the Rebellion, 128 Volumes. Washington, D.C.: Government Printing Office, 1880–1896.

ToxFAQs for Mercury, Agency for Toxic Substances and Disease Registry. Available at http://www.atskr.cdc.gov/tfacts46.html#bookmark04.

Published Primary Sources

Adams, Charles Francis. *Charles Francis Adams: An Autobiography.* Boston: Houghton Mifflin Company, 1916.

Bennitt, M. D., John. *"I Hope to Do My Country Service:" The Civil War Letters of John Bennitt, M. D., Surgeon, 19th Michigan Infantry.* Edited by Robert Beasecker. Detroit, Michigan: Wayne State University Press, 2005.

Butler, Benjamin Franklin. *Autobiography and personal reminiscences of Major-General Benjamin F. Butler: Butler's Book.* A. M. Thayer: 1892.

Butterfield, Daniel. *A Biographical Memorial of General Daniel Butterfield: Including Many Addresses and Military Writings.* Edited by Julia Lorrilard Butterfield. New York: Grafton Press, 1904.

Chesnut, Mary. *Mary Chesnut's Civil War.* Edited by C. Vann Woodward. Connecticut: Yale University Press, 1981.

Custer, Elizabeth Bacon. *The Civil War Memories of Elizabeth Bacon Custer: Reconstructed From Her Notes and Diaries.* Edited by Arlene Reynolds. Austin: University of Texas Press, 1994.

Davis, W. W. "Cavalry Service under General Wheeler." *Confederate Veteran Magazine,* August 1903, 353.

Davis, W. W. "Kilpatrick's Spotted Horse." *Confederate Veteran Magazine,* February 1906, 62.

Dyer, J. Franklin. *The Journal of a Civil War Surgeon.* Edited by Michael B. Chesson. Lincoln: University of Nebraska Press, 2003.

Edwards, Madaline Selima. *Madaline: Love and Survival in Antebellum New Orleans.* Edited by Dell Upton. Athens: University of Georgia Press, 1996.

Fancher, Jefferson B., M.D. *Medical, Matrimonial, and Scientific Expositor; Giving the Most Important Information Upon Every Subject Relating to Man and Woman.* New York: Author, 1867.

Grant, Ulysses S. *The Personal Memoirs of Ulysses S. Grant.* Old Sybrook, CT: Konecky & Konecky, 1992.

Kidd, James H. *One of Custer's Wolverines: The Civil War Letters of Brevet Brigadier General James H. Kidd, 6th Michigan Cavalry.* Edited by Eric J. Wittenberg. Kent, OH: Kent State University Press, 2000.

Letterman, Jonathan. *Medical Recollections of the Army of the Potomac.* D. Appleton and Company, 1866.

McAllister, Robert. *The Civil War Letters of General Robert McAllister.* Edited by James I. Robertson, Jr. New Brunswick, NJ: Rutgers University Press, 1965.

Molyneax, Joel. *Quill of the Wild Goose: Civil War Letters and Diaries of Private Joel Molyneax, 141st. P. V.* Edited by Kermit Molyneax. Shuppensburg, PA: Burd Street Press, 1996.

Moss, Lemuel. *Annals of the U.S. Christian Commission.* Philadelphia: J.B. Lippincott & Co., 1868.

Parton, James. General *Butler in New Orleans: History of the Administration of the Department of the Gulf in the Year 1862: With an Account of the Capture of New Orleans and a Sketch of the Previous Career of the General, Civil, and Military.* New York: Mason Brothers, 1864.

Patrick, Marsena Rudolph. *Inside Lincoln's Army: The Diary of Marsena Rudoph Patrick, Provost Marshal General.* Edited by David S. Sparks. New York: A. S. Barnes and Company, 1964.

Pope, John. *The Military Memoirs of General John Pope.* Edited by Peter Cozzens and Robert I Girardi. Chapel Hill: University of North Carolina Press, 1998.

Scherneckau, August. *Marching with the First Nebraska: A Civil War Diary.* Edited by James E. Potter and Edith Robbins. Norman: University of Oklahoma Press, 2007.

Sipple, Thomas. Letter to President Abraham Lincoln, August 1864. In *Free at Last: A Documentary History of Slavery, Freedom, and the Civil War.* Edited by Ira Berlin et al. New York City: New Press, 1992.

Smith, Edward P. *Incidents of the United States Christian Commission.* Philadelphia: J. B. Lippincott & Co., 1871.

Smith, Edward P. *Thrilling Incidents of the War: The Only Authentic Work Extant Giving the Many Tragic and Touching Incidents That Came Under the Notice of the United States Christian Commission During the Long Years of the War.* n.p., 1868.

Soldiers from the 33rd USCT. Letter to General Daniel Sickles, January 1866. In *Freedom's Soldiers: The Black Military Experience in the Civil War.* Edited by Ira Berlin, Joseph P. Reidy, and Leslie S. Rowland. New York City: Cambridge University Press, 1998.

Springer, Francis. *The Preacher's Tale: The Civil War Journal of Rev. Francis Springer, Chaplain, US Army of the Frontier.* Edited by William Furry. Fayetteville: University of Arkansas Press, 2001.

Stille, Charles Janeway. *History of the United States Sanitary Commission, Being the General Report of its Work During the War of the Rebellion.* Philadelphia: J. B. Lippincott & Co., 1866.

Strong, George Templeton. *The Diary of George Templeton Strong: Post-War Years, 1865–1875.* New York: The Macmillan Company, 1952.

Todd, John. *The Young Man: Hints Addressed to the Young Men of the United States.* Northhampton, PA: J. H. Butler, 1845.

Tubbs, Charles. *Mr. Tubbs' Civil War.* Edited by Nat Brandt. Syracuse, NY: Syracuse University Press, 1996.

Unsigned. Letter to unnamed official, August 1864. In *Freedom's Soldiers: The Black Military Experience in the Civil War.* Edited by Ira Berlin, Joseph P. Reidy, and Leslie S. Rowland. New York City: Cambridge University Press, 1998.

US Christian Comm. Instructions to Delegates of the U.S. Christian
    Commission. Philadelphia: n.p., 1862.

Watkins, Sam R. *Co. Aytch: A Confederate Memoir of the Civil War.* New York:
    MacMillan Publishers, 1962. Reprint, New York: Touchstone, 1997.

Wilson, Ephraim A. *Memoirs of the War by Captain Ephraim A. Wilson, of Co.
    "G," 10th Illinois Veteran Volunteer Infantry.* Cleveland: W. M. Bayne
    Printing Co., 1893.

Secondary Sources

Barber, Susan. "Depraved and Abandoned Women: Prostitution in Richmond,
    Virginia, across the Civil War." In *Neither Lady nor Slave: Working Women
    of the Old South.* Edited by Susanna Delfino and Michele Gillespie. Chapel
    Hill: University of North Carolina Press, 2002.

Bennett, Michael J. *Union Jacks: Yankee Sailors in the Civil War.* Chapel Hill:
    University of North Carolina Press, 2003.

Bergeron, Paul H., Stephen V. Ash, and Jeanette Keith. *Tennesseans and Their
    History.* Knoxville: University of Tennessee Press, 1999.

Bradley, Michael R. *With Blood and Fire: Life behind Union Lines in Middle
    Tennessee, 1863–65.* Shippensburg, PA: Burd Street Press, 2003.

Bremmer, Robert H. *The Public Good: Philanthropy and Welfare in the Civil
    War Era.* New York: Alfred A. Knopf, 1980.

"Britain to delete term 'prostitute' from law books." Available at http://today
    .reuters.com.

Brock, Darla. "Memphis's Nymphs Du Pave: 'The Most Abandoned Women
    in the World." In *West Tennessee Historical Society's Papers 50.* Memphis:
    West Tennessee Historical Society, 1996.

Butler, Anne M. *Daughters of Joy, Sisters of Misery: Prostitutes in the
    American West, 1865–90.* Urbana: University of Illinois Press, 1985.

Bynum, Victoria E. *Unruly Women: The Politics of Social and Sexual Control
    in the Old South.* Chapel Hill: University of North Carolina Press, 1992.

Cayleff, Susan E. *Wash and Be Healed: The Water-Cure Movement and
    Women's Health.* Philadelphia: Temple University Press, 1987.

Clinton, Catherine. "'Public Women,' and Sexual Politics during the American
    Civil War." In *Battle Scars: Gender and Sexuality in the American Civil
    War.* Edited by Catherine Clinton and Nina Silber, 61–77. New York:
    Oxford University Press, 2006.

Clinton, Catherine. *Public Women and the Confederacy.* Milwaukee: Marquette
    University Press, 1999.

Cohen, Patricia Cline. *The Murder of Helen Jewett: The Life and Death of a
    Prostitute in Nineteenth Century New York.* New York: Alfred A. Knopf,
    Inc., 1998.

Cooper, William J., and Thomas E. Terrill. *The American South: A History,* 3rd ed. Boston: McGraw Hill, 2002.

Cunningham, Horace Herndon. *Doctors in Gray: The Confederate Medical Service.* Baton Rouge: Louisiana State University Press, 1958.

Davis, Burke. *The Civil War: Strange & Fascinating Facts.* New York: Wings Books, 1960. Repr., Austin: Holt, Rinehart, and Winston, Inc, 1996.

"Disneyland East." *Time Magazine,* 6 May 1966. Available at: http://www.time .com/magazine/article/0,9171,901833,00.html.

Dyer, John P. *The Gallant Hood.* New York: Konecky & Konecky, 1950.

Edwards, Laura F. *Scarlett Doesn't Live Here Anymore: Southern Women in the Civil War Era.* Urbana: University of Illinois Press, 2000.

Faust, Drew Gilpin. *Mothers of Invention: Women of the Slaveholeing South in the American Civil War.* Chapel Hill: University of North Carolina Press, 1996.

Foreman, Michael D. "The Secession of Franklin County." In *Franklin County Historical Review: The War of 1861–1865, A Franklin County Perspective,* 28 (1998): 2–16.

Freemon, Frank R. *Gangrene and Glory: Medical Care during the American Civil War.* Cranbury, NJ: Associated University Presses, 1998.

Furguson, Ernest B. *Ashes of Glory: Richmond at War.* New York: Alfred A. Knopf, 1996.

———. *Freedom Rising: Washington in the Civil War.* New York: Alfred A. Knopf, 2004.

Gilfoyle, Timothy. *City of Eros: New York City, Prostitution, and the Commercialization of Sex, 1790–1920.* New York: W. W. Norton & Co., 1994.

Ginzberg, Lori D. *Women and the Work of Benevolence: Morality, Politics, and Class in the Nineteenth-Century United States.* New Haven, CT: Yale University Press, 1990.

Glatthaar, Joseph T. "The Costliness of Discrimination: Medical Care for Black Troops in the Civil War." In *Inside the Confederate Nation: Essays in Honor of Emory M. Thomas.* Edited by Lesley J. Gordon and John C. Inscoe, 251–271. Baton Rouge: Louisiana State University Press, 2005.

Gross, Jennifer Lynn. "And for the Widow & Orphan? Confederate Widows, Poverty, & Public Assistance." In *Inside the Confederate Nation: Essays in Honor of Emory M. Thomas.* Edited by Lesley J. Gordon and John C. Inscoe. Baton Rouge: Louisiana State University Press, 2005.

Halttunen, Karen. *Confidence Men and Painted Women: A Study of Middle-Class Culture in America, 1830–1870.* New Haven, CT: Yale University Press, 1982.

Hannah, Howard Malcolm. "Confederate Action in Franklin County, Tennessee." In *Franklin County Historical Review* 23 (1992): 2–4.

Hearn, Chester G. *When the Devil Came Down to Dixie: Ben Butler in New Orleans.* Baton Rouge: Louisiana State University Press, 1997.

Herbert, Walter H. *Fighting Joe Hooker.* Lincoln: University of Nebraska Press, 1999.

Hoffert Sylvia D. *A History of Gender in America: Essays, Documents, and Articles.* Upper Saddle River, NJ: Prentice Hall, 2003.

Horowitz, Helen Lefkowitz. *Attitudes toward Sex in Antebellum America: A Brief History with Documents.* Boston: Bedford/St. Martins, 2006.

———. *Rereading Sex: Battles over Sexual Knowledge and Suppression in Nineteenth-Century America.* New York: Alfred A. Knopf, 2002.

Houghton, Walter E. *The Victorian Frame of Mind, 1830–1870.* New Haven, CT: Yale University Press, 1957.

Jones, Jr., James Boyd. "A Tale of Two Cities: The Hidden Battle against Venereal Disease in Civil War Nashville and Memphis." *Civil War History* 31 (September 1985): 270–276.

———. "Municipal Vice: The Management of Prostitution in Tennessee's Urban Experience. Part I: The Experience of Nashville and Memphis, 1854–1917." *Tennessee Historical Quarterly 50* (1991): 33–41.

Keneally, Thomas. *American Scoundrel: The Life of the Notorious Civil War General Dan Sickles.* New York: Nan A. Talese, 2002.

Lebsock, Suzanne. *The Free Women of Petersburg: Status and Culture in a Southern Town, 1784–1860.* New York: W. W. Norton & Company, 1984.

Leech, Margaret. *Reveille in Washington, 1860–1865.* New York: Carroll & Graf Publishers, Inc., 1941.

Leonard, Elizabeth D. *All the Daring of the Soldier: Women of the Civil War Armies.* New York: W. W. Norton & Co., 1999.

———. *Yankee Women: Gender Battles in the Civil War.* New York: W. W. Norton & Co., 1995.

"Lifesaving Politics." *Ms. Magazine,* Spring 2007: 12–13.

Linderman, Gerald. *Embattled Courage: The Experience of Combat in the American Civil War.* New York: The Free Press, 1987.

Long, Alecia P. *The Great Southern Babylon: Sex, Race and Respectability in New Orleans, 1865–1920.* Baton Rouge: Louisiana State University Press, 2004.

Longacre, Edward. *The Commanders of Chancellorsville: The Gentleman vs. The Rogue.* Nashville: Rutledge Hill Press, 2005.

Lowry, Thomas P. *The Civil War Bawdy Houses of Washington, D.C.* Fredericksburg, Virginia: Sergeant Kirkland's Museum and Historical Society, Inc., 1997.

———. *The Story the Soldiers Wouldn't Tell: Sex in the Civil War.* Mechanicsburg, PA: Stackpole Books, 1994.

Martin, Samuel J. *Kill-Cavalry: The Life of Union General Hugh Judson Kilpatrick.* Mechanicsburg, PA: Stackpole Books, 2000.

Maxwell, William Quentin. *Lincoln's Fifth Wheel: The Political History of the United States Sanitary Commission.* New York: Longmans, Green, 1956.

McDevitt, Theresa. "Fighting for the Soul of America: A History of the United States Christian Commission." Ph.D. dissertation, Kent State University, 1997.

McPherson, James M. *For Cause & Comrades: Why Men Fought in the Civil War.* New York: Oxford University Press, 1997.

————. *Ordeal by Fire: The Civil War and Reconstruction,* 3rd ed. Boston: McGraw Hill, 2001.

Mitchell, Reid. *Civil War Soldiers.* New York: Viking Penguin Books, 1988. Repr., New York: Penguin Books, 1997.

Murphy, Lawrence. "The Enemy among Us: Venereal Disease among Union Soldiers in the Far West, 1861–1865." In *Civil War History* 31 (1985): 257–269.

Musicant, Ivan. *Divided Waters: The Naval History of the Civil War.* New York: Harper Collins Publishers, 1995.

O'Connor, Thomas H. *Civil War Boston: Home Front & Battlefield.* Boston: Northeastern University Press, 1997.

Orchitis. MayoClinic.com. Available at http://www.mayoclinic.com/health/orchitis/DS00602.

Parks, Joseph H. *General Leonidas Polk, C. S. A.: The Fighting Bishop.* Baton Rouge: Louisiana State University Press, 1962.

Perman, Michael ed. *Major Problems in the Civil War and Reconstruction.* Lexington, MA: D.C. Heath and Company, 1991.

Rable, George C. *Civil Wars: Women and the Crisis of Southern Nationalism.* Urbana: University of Illinois Press, 1989.

Radley, Kenneth. *Rebel Watchdog: The Confederate States Army Provost Guard.* Baton Rouge: Louisiana State University Press, 1989.

Ramold, Steven J. *Slaves, Sailors, Citizens: African Americans in the Union Navy.* DeKalb: Northern Illinois University Press, 2002.

Robertson, Jr., James I. *Soldiers Blue and Gray.* Columbia: University of South Carolina Press, 1998.

Rosen, Ruth. *The Lost Sisterhood: Prostitution in America 1900–1918.* Baltimore, MD: Johns Hopkins University Press, 1982.

Seagraves, Anne. *Soiled Doves: Prostitution in the Early West.* Hayden, ID: Wesanne Publications, 1994.

Sears, Stephen W. *George B. McClellan: The Young Napoleon.* Boston: Ticknor and Fields, 1988. Reprint, New York: De Capo Press, 1999.

Sexual Transmitted Diseases Guide: Online Version. Available at: http://std-gov.org/stds/gonorrhea.htm.

Srebnick, Amy Gilman. *The Mysterious Death of Mary Rogers: Sex and Culture in Nineteenth-Century New York.* New York: Oxford University Press, 1995.

Stansell, Christine. *City of Women: Sex and Class in New York: 1789–1860*. Champaign: University of Illinois Press, 1987.

Swanberg, W. A. *Sickles the Incredible*. New York: Charles Scribner's Sons, 1956.

Topping, Elizabeth P. *What's a Poor Girl To Do? Prostitution in Mid-Nineteenth Century America*. Gettysburg, PA: Thomas Publications, 2001.

Wagner, Margaret E., Gary W. Gallagher, and Paul Finkelman, eds. *The Library of Congress Civil War Desk Reference*. New York: Simon & Schuster, 2002.

Walters, Ronald G. *American Reformers, 1815–1860*. New York: Hill and Wang, 1978.

Waugh, John C. *The Class of 1846: From West Point to Appomattox: Stonewall Jackson, George McClellan and their Brothers*. New York: Ballantine Publishing Group, 1994.

West, Carroll Van, ed. *Tennessee History: The Land, the People, and the Culture*. Knoxville: University of Tennessee Press, 1998.

Wiley, Bell I. *The Life of Billy Yank*. Indianapolis: Bobbs-Merrill Company, 1951.

———. *The Life of Johnny Reb*. Indianapolis: Bobbs-Merrill Company, 1943.

———. *Confederate Women: Beyond the Petticoat*. Westport, CT: Greenwood Publishing, 1975. Repr., New York: Barnes & Noble Press, 1994.

Woloch, Nancy. *Women and the American Experience*, 4th ed. Boston: McGraw Hill, 2006.

Woodworth, Steven E. *While God Is Marching On: The Religious World of Civil War Soldiers*. Lawrence: University Press of Kansas, 2001.

Wusch, James. "The Social Evil Ordinance." *American Heritage Magazine*, 33 no. 2 (1982). Accessed February 25, 2009 at http://www.americanheritage.com/articles/magazine/ah/1982/2/1982_2_50_print.shtml.

Index

CPSIA information can be obtained at www.ICGtesting.com
Printed in the USA
LVOW12s0848090415

433695LV00005B/35/P